Sealed from Within:
Self-Authenticating Insular Charters

DAVID HOWLETT

From original manuscripts David Howlett edits, translates, and analyses twenty-four Latin charters – English, Welsh, Cornish, Irish, Scottish, and Hebridean – from the 7th century to the 15th, as monuments of thought and composition parallel to the literary and epigraphic traditions of these islands. This revolutionary analysis presents charters of local variety but underlying unity, in which complex self-authenticating mathematical structures produce works of art of astonishing and apprehensible beauty.

David Howlett is the author of *The Book of Letters of Saint Patrick the Bishop* (1994), *The Celtic Latin Tradition of Biblical Style* (1995), *The English Origins of Old French Literature* (1996), *British Books in Biblical Style* (1997) and *Cambro-Latin Compositions: Their Competence and Craftsmanship* (1998). Forthcoming is *Pillars of Wisdom: Irishmen, Englishmen, Liberal Arts*.

Sealed from Within

Self-Authenticating Insular Charters

DAVID HOWLETT

FOUR COURTS PRESS

Typeset in 10.5 pt on 12 pt Bembo by
Carrigboy Typesetting Services, County Cork for
FOUR COURTS PRESS LTD
Fumbally Court, Fumbally Lane, Dublin 8, Ireland
e-mail: info@four-courts-press.ie
and in North America for
FOUR COURTS PRESS
c/o ISBS, 5804 N.E. Hassalo Street, Portland, OR 97213.

A catalogue record for this title is available
from the British Library.

ISBN 1-85182-455-3

The device on the case of this book is based on a drawing
of a sign manual in MS Cotton Augustus II.2 and is
used with the permission of the British Library.

Printed in Great Britain
by Antony Rowe Ltd, Chippenham, Wilts.

For

Pierre Chaplais

and for

Simon Keynes

De uerbo in uerbum legi et diligenter examinaui

CONTENTS

PROLOGUE

In a thesis and a series of books and articles I have identified some elements of a mode of thought and composition derived from the Hebrew Old Testament and the Greek New Testament, perfectly reproduced in the Vulgate Latin Bible, transmitted from Late Latin authors to Romano-British authors of the fifth century, and from them to thousands of writers in Insular Latin (men of Celtic, Germanic, and Romance mother tongues), Old Welsh, Old Irish, Old English, Old Norse, and Old French, all of which literatures came into existence in these islands.[1] Parallel to this tradition of manuscript literature and simultaneous with it is a tradition of Insular inscriptions on stone.[2] The purpose of the present

1 D.R. Howlett, *Studies in the Works of John Whethamstede*, University of Oxford D.Phil. thesis (1975); *Liber Epistolarum Sancti Patricii Episcopi: The Book of Letters of Saint Patrick the Bishop* (Dublin: Four Courts, 1994); *The Celtic Latin Tradition of Biblical Style* (Dublin: Four Courts, 1995); *The English Origins of Old French Literature* (Dublin: Four Courts, 1996); *British Books in Biblical Style* (Dublin: Four Courts, 1997); *Cambro-Latin Compositions: Their Competence and Craftsmanship* (Dublin: Four Courts, 1998); *Caledonian Craftsmanship: The Scottish Latin Tradition* (Dublin: Four Courts, 1999 forthcoming); *Pillars of Wisdom: Irishmen, Englishmen, Liberal Arts* (Dublin: Four Courts, 2000 forthcoming); 'Some Criteria for Editing Abaelard', *Archivum Latinitatis Medii Aevi* LI (1992–3), pp. 195–202; 'Aldhelm and Irish Learning', *Ibid.* LII (1994), pp. 37–75; '*Aldhelmi Carmen Rhythmicum*', *Ibid.* LIII (1995), pp. 119–40; 'Miscouplings in Couplets', *Ibid.* LV (1997), pp. 271–6; 'Arithmetic Rhythms in Latin Letters, *Ibid.* LVI (1998) pp. 193–225; 'Two Works of Saint Columban', *Mittellateinisches Jahrbuch* XXVIII (1994 for 1993), pp. 27–46; 'Numerical Play in Wulfstan's Verse and Prose', *Ibid.* XXXI (1996), pp. 61–7; 'Sixes and Sevens in Anglo-Latin Prologues', *Ibid.* (forthcoming); 'The Earliest Irish Writers at Home and Abroad', *Peritia* VIII (1994), pp. 1–17; 'Five Experiments in Textual Reconstruction and Analysis', *Ibid.* IX (1995), pp. 1–50; 'Seven Studies in Seventh-Century Texts', *Ibid.* X (1996), pp. 1–70; '*Rubisca*: An Edition, Translation, and Commentary', *Ibid.*, pp. 71–90; 'Insular Latin Writers' Rhythms', *Ibid.* XI (1997), pp. 53–116; '*Vita I Sanctae Brigitae*', *Ibid.* XII (1998), pp. 1–23; 'Insular Acrostics, Celtic Latin Colophons', *Cambrian Medieval Celtic Studies* XXXV (1998), pp. 27–44; 'The Literary Context of Geoffrey of Monmouth: An Essay on the Fabrication of Sources', *Arthuriana* V.III (1995), pp. 25–69.

2 R.A.S. Macalister, *Corpus Inscriptionum Insularum Celticarum*, 2 vols (Dublin: Stationery Office, 1945, 1949, vol. I rept with a preface by Damian McManus, Dublin: Four Courts and Irish Manuscripts Commission, 1996). V.E. Nash-Williams, *The Early Christian Monuments of Wales* (Cardiff: University of Wales Press, 1950). Charles

book is to demonstrate that Insular diplomatic practice among Englishmen, Welshmen, Cornishmen, Irishmen, Scotsmen, and Hebrideans conformed in local variety but underlying unity with this tradition of thought and composition from the seventh century to the fifteenth.[3]

ACKNOWLEDGEMENTS

I owe thanks to Dauvit Broun, Pierre Chaplais, Thomas Charles-Edwards, David Dumville, Anthony Harvey, Leofranc Holford-Strevens, and Simon Keynes for learning generously shared and for helpful criticism.

Thomas, *Britain and Ireland in Early Christian Times, AD 400–800* (London: Thames and Hudson, 1971); *The Early Christian Archaeology of North Britain* (London: Oxford University Press for the University of Glasgow, 1971); *Christianity in Roman Britain to AD 500* (Berkeley and Los Angeles: University of California Press, 1981); *Whithorn's Christian Beginnings*, First Whithorn Lecture (Whithorn: Friends of the Whithorn Trust, 1992); 'The Early Christian Inscriptions of Southern Scotland', *Glasgow Archaeological Journal* XVII (1994 for 1991–2), pp. 1–10; 'The Llanddewi-Brefi "Idnert" Stone', *Peritia* X (1996), pp. 136–83; 'The Conversions of Scotland', The John Jamieson Lecture, *Records of the Scottish Church History Society* XXVII (1997), pp. 1–41; 'Christian Latin Inscriptions from Cornwall in Biblical Style', *Journal of the Royal Institution of Cornwall*, New Series II.II.IV (1997), pp. 42–66; *Christian Celts: Messages and Images* (Stroud: Tempus, 1998); *The Penzance Market Cross* (Penzance: Penlee House Gallery and Museum, 1999). David Howlett, 'Inscriptions and Design of the Ruthwell Cross' in *The Ruthwell Cross*, ed. Brendan Cassidy (Princeton University Press, 1992), pp. 71–93; Cassidy and Howlett, 'Some Eighteenth-Century Drawings of the Ruthwell Cross', *The Antiquaries Journal* LXXII (1992), pp. 102–17; Howlett, *Cambro-Latin Compositions*, pp. 17–32.

3 Some of the features analysed in the charters are represented in the book: 7 words and 7 x 7 letters in the title, 7 chapters in the book, 24 words from the title to the dedication inclusive and 24 charters analysed, 30 words in the acknowledgements, 365 words and numbers (excluding page numbers) in the contents, 46 syllables from the title to the dedication inclusive, 153 words in the prologue, 1111 words in the epilogue.

I

RULES AND ADJUNCTS OF BIBLICAL STYLE

I. RULES OF BIBLICAL STYLE

Biblical style is iterative; it consists in stating an idea and then restating it (as in this sentence). One finds Scriptural warrant for such an iterative style in Ecclesiasticus XLII 24:[1]

> παντα δισσα εν κατεναντι του ενος
> και ουκ εποιησεν ουδεν ελλειπον

rendered in the Vulgate at XLII 25:

> omnia duplicia unum contra unum
> et non fecit quicquam deesse,

and in English:

> all things are twofold, one opposite the other,
> and He has made nothing incomplete.

There are three primary patterns of iteration. In the smallest unit of Biblical style, the structure of a single verse, the first and basic pattern is parallelism, a statement followed by a restatement in identical order, as Isaiah I 10:

e d c b a
שִׁמְע֥וּ דְבַר־יְהוָ֖ה קְצִינֵ֣י סְדֹ֑ם
e' d' c' b' a'
הַאֲזִ֛ינוּ תּוֹרַ֥ת אֱלֹהֵ֖ינוּ עַ֥ם עֲמֹרָֽה׃

a b c d e
ακουσατε λογον Κυριου αρχοντες Σοδομων.
a' b' c' d' e'
προσεχετε νομον Θεου λαος Γομορρας.

1 Biblical quotations are taken in Hebrew from *Biblia Hebraica Stuttgartensia*, ed. K. Elliger *et al.* (Stuttgart: Württembergische Bibelanstalt, 1969–76); in Greek from *Septuaginta*,

a b c d e
audite uerbum Domini principes Sodomorum
a' b' c' d' e'
percipite auribus legem Dei nostri populus Gomorrae.
a b c d e
Hear the word of the Lord, you rulers of Sodom.
a' b c' d' e'
Give ear to the teaching of our God, you people of Gomorrah.

An example in English nursery rhyme is

To market, to market, to buy a fat pig,
home again, home again, jiggety jig.
To market, to market, to buy a fat hog,
home again, home again, jiggety jog.

The second but still basic pattern, which also appears in the structure of a single verse, is chiasmus, a statement followed by a restatement in reverse order, as Lamentations I 1:

aii ai
הָיְתָה כְּאַלְמָנָה
bii bi
רַבָּתִי בַגּוֹיִם
b'ii b'i
שָׂרָתִי בַּמְּדִינוֹת
a'ii a'i
הָיְתָה לָמַס׃ ס

ai aii
εγενηθη ως χηρα
bi bii
πεπληθυμμενη εν εθνεσιν
b'i b'ii
αρχουσα εν χωραις
a'i a'ii
εγενηθη εις φορον

ed. A. Rahlfs (Stuttgart: Deutsche Bibelstiftung, 1935) and *The Greek New Testament*, ed. K. Aland *et al.*, ed. 3 corr. (Stuttgart: United Bible Societies, 1983); in Latin from *Biblia Sacra iuxta Vulgatam Versionem*, ed. B. Fischer *et al.* (Stuttgart: Württembergische Bibelanstalt, 1969); and in English from the Revised Standard Version, ed. 2, with occasional changes of word order to reflect the order of original texts. Parallel indentations and superscript letters, as well as letters and numbers in the margin, are intended to show what words and phrases are paired.

a i a ii		
facta est quasi uidua	a	How like a widow she has become
b i b ii		
domina gentium	b	she that was great among the nations;
b'i b'ii		
princeps prouinciarum	b'	she that was a princess among the cities
a'i a'ii		
facta est sub tributo	a'	has become a vassal.

An example in English nursery rhyme is

As I was going to Saint Ives
I met a man with seven wives;
each wife had seven sacks;
each sack had seven cats;
each cat had seven kits.
Kits,
cats,
sacks,
and wives,
how many were going to Saint Ives?

John Henry Newman's hymn is in the same form:

Praise to the Holiest
in the height
and in the depth
be praise,
in all His words
most wonderful,
most sure
in all His ways.

Moving on to a larger unit, which extends to several verses, the third pattern combines parallelism and chiasmus, as Amos II 14–6:

a*a* וְאָבַד מָנוֹס מִקָּל
b*b* וְחָזָק לֹא־יְאַמֵּץ כֹּחוֹ
c*c* וְגִבּוֹר לֹא־יְמַלֵּט נַפְשׁוֹ׃
d*d* וְתֹפֵשׂ הַקֶּשֶׁת לֹא יַעֲמֹד
d' *a'* וְקַל בְּרַגְלָיו לֹא יְמַלֵּט
c' *b'* וְרֹכֵב הַסּוּס לֹא יְמַלֵּט נַפְשׁוֹ׃
b' *c'* וְאַמִּיץ לִבּוֹ בַּגִּבּוֹרִים
a' *d'* עָרוֹם יָנוּס בַּיּוֹם־הַהוּא נְאֻם־יְהוָה׃ פ

a *a* “And flight shall perish from the swift
b *b* and the strong shall not retain his strength
c *c* and the mighty shall not save his life
d *d* and he who handles the bow shall not stand
d' *a'* and he who is swift of foot shall not save himself
c' *b'* and he who rides the horse shall not save his life
b' *c'* and he who is stout of heart among the mighty
a' *d'* shall flee away naked in that day,” says the Lord.

Note in a and a' the second words מָנוֹס 'flight' and יָנוּס 'he shall flee'; in b the penultimate word יְאַמֵּץ 'strengthen' and in b' the first word וְאַמִּיץ 'and the strong'; in c and c' the identical concluding phrase לֹא־יְמַלֵּט נַפְשׁוֹ 'shall not save his life'; in d and d' the similar concluding phrases לֹא יַעֲמֹד 'shall not stand' and לֹא יְמַלֵּט 'shall not save himself'. This makes a clear and consistent chiasmus. But there is also a parallelism. The last word of *a*, מִקָּל 'from the swift', is echoed by the first word of *a'* וְקַל 'and the swift'. The first word of *c*, וְגִבּוֹר 'and the mighty', is echoed by the last word of *c'*, בַּגִּבּוֹרִים 'among the mighty'.

Here is the Septuagint text of the same verses.

a*a* και απολειται φυγη εκ δρομεως
b*b* και ο κραταιος ου μη κρατησηι της ισχυος αυτου
c*c* και ο μαχητης ου μη σωσηι την ψυχην αυτου
d*d* και ο τοξοτης ου μη υποστηι
d'*a'* και ο οξυς τοις ποσιν αυτου ου μη διασωθηι
c'*b'* ουδε ο ιππευς ου μη σωσηι την ψυχην αυτου
b'*c'* και ευρησει την καρδιαν αυτου εν δυναστειαις
a'*d'* ο γυμνος διωξεται εν εκεινηι τηι ημεραι λεγει Κυριος

The chiasmus is partly reproduced. Note, for example, in c and c' the identical concluding phrase ου μη σωσηι την ψυχην αυτου and in d and d' the similar concluding phrases ου μη υποστηι and ου μη διασωθηι. Rahlfs rejected a variant reading of b', ο κραταιος ου μη ευρη, because there is no warrant in the Hebrew text for the negative. The reading does not reflect the original, but it is valuable evidence that some Greek-speaking editor or scribe recognized and tried to improve the chiasmus, making ο κραταιος ου μη ευρη or ευρησει a clearer parallel to ο κραταιος ου μη κρατησηι. The translator of this part of the Septuagint has rendered the chiasmus only imperfectly, and he has not reproduced the parallelism at all.

When we look at the Vulgate, however, we see that Jerome has reproduced both chiasmus and parallelism well.

a*a*	et peribit fuga a ueloce
b*b*	et fortis non obtinebit uirtutem suam
c*c*	et robustus non saluabit animam suam
d*d*	et tenens arcum non stabit
d'*a'*	et uelox pedibus suis non saluabitur
c'*b'*	et ascensor equi non saluabit animam suam
b'*c'*	et robustus corde inter fortes
a'*d'*	nudus fugiet in die illa dicit Dominus.

He balances *fuga* in a with *fugiet* in a', uses the same concluding phrase at the ends of c and c', *non saluabit animam suam*, and similar concluding phrases at the ends of d and d', *non stabit* and *non saluabitur*. He even improves the chiasmus by making the last words of b', *inter fortes*, echo the first words of b, *et fortis*. But he also reproduces the parallelism, echoing the last words of *a*, *a ueloce*, with the first words of *a'*, *et uelox*, and repeating *et robustus* at the beginnings of *c* and *c'*.

Let us consider a fourth paradigm, from the New Testament, Saint John's Gospel, which begins with a chiastic and parallel Prologue (1 1–5):

A 1	In the beginning	Εν αρχηι
2	was	ην
3	the Word,	ο λογος
4	and the Word	και ο λογος
5	was	ην
6	with God	προς τον Θεον
7	and	και
6'	God	Θεος
5'	was	ην
4'	the Word;	ο λογος
3'	He	ουτος
2'	was	ην
1'	in the beginning with God.	εν αρχηι προς τον Θεον.
B 1	All things	Παντα
2	through Him were made	δια αυτου εγενετο
3	and	και
2'	without Him was made	χωρις αυτου εγενετο
1'	not one thing.	ουδε εν.
C 1	What was made in Him	Ο γεγονεν εν αυτωι
2	life was	ζωη ην
3	and	και
2'	the life was	η ζωη ην
1'	the light of men.	το φως των ανθρωπων.
D 1	And the light in the darkness shines	Και το φως εν τηι σκοτιαι φαινει
1'	and the darkness has not overcome it.	και η σκοτια αυτο ου κατελαβεν.

A1 In principio
2 erat
3 Verbum
4 et Verbum
5 erat
6 apud Deum
7 et
6' Deus
5' erat
4' Verbum;
3' Hoc
2 erat
1' in principio apud Deum.
B1 Omnia
2 per ipsum facta sunt
3 et
2' sine ipso factum est
1' nihil.
C1 Quod factum est in ipso
2 uita erat
3 et
2' uita erat
1' lux hominum.
D1 Et lux in tenebris lucet
1' et tenebrae eam non comprehenderunt.

In A the author's ideas at the beginning of the first half, 'In the beginning', and at the end of the first half, 'with God', are restated together at the end of the second half, 'in the beginning with God'. Everything else is chiastically disposed. Compare 'was' in 2 with 'was' in 2', 'the Word' in 3 with 'He, the same' in 3', 'the Word' in 4 with 'the Word' in 4', 'was' in 5 with 'was' in 5', 'with God' in 6 with 'God' in 6', around the central 'and' 7.

Again the author writes chiastically in B, balancing 'all things' in 1 with 'not one thing' in 1' and 'through Him came into being' in 2 with 'without Him came into being' in 2' around the central 'and' in 3.

Yet again he writes chiastically in C, balancing 'what came into being through Him' in 1 with 'the light of men' in 1' and 'life was' in 2 with 'the life was' in 2' around the central 'and' in 3.

Finally he writes parallel in D, 'And the light in the shadows shines, and the shadows have not comprehended [or "grasped" or "overcome"] it'.

Observe the incremental unfolding of ideas. First the author defines his subject as one with God twice. Second he combines αυτου with εγενετο twice. Third he puts αυτωι and γεγονεν together with ζωη 'life' twice, which he describes as φως 'light'. Fourth he contrasts light with darkness twice. His thought runs first 'in the beginning God', second 'He being or becoming or making', third 'He begetting life', 'life light', and fourth 'light shining triumphant'. Ten of the verbs are past, aorist, or perfect, but this one, φαινει, is present.

These chiastic and parallel structures, coinciding exactly with the statement and incremental restatement of ideas, are as clear as they could possibly be. There is not the slightest doubt about where they begin and where they end, nor about what they say. But there is more to them than this.

Counting the words in A one finds twenty-four, arranged twelve and twelve. In B there are ten, arranged five and five. In C there are fourteen, arranged seven and seven. In D there are thirteen, of which the seventh and central is the one present tense verb of the entire passage, φαινει.

There is more. Counting the syllables one finds in A thirty-three, arranged sixteen, one, sixteen. In B there are twenty-two syllables, arranged eleven and eleven. In C there are twenty-one syllables, arranged eleven and ten. In D there are twenty-three syllables, eleven in the first clause and twelve in the second. These symmetries of word and syllable are apprehensible by ear. But there are more, apprehensible only by the eye.

Counting the letters one finds in A seventy-seven, arranged thirty-seven, three, and thirty-seven. In B there are forty-six letters arranged twenty-three and twenty-three. In C there are forty-five letters arranged twenty-three and twenty-two. In D there are twenty-six letters in the first clause and twenty-five in the second. But if we followed the variant reading αυτον, assuming that the antecedent was masculine λογος or ουτος or αυτος rather than neuter φως, there would be twenty-six letters in the first clause and twenty-six in the second.

All these symmetries are either perfect or within one of perfection.[2] The author gets and holds our attention with chiastic and parallel statement and incremental restatement, and whether we consider ideas or numbers of words or numbers of syllables or numbers of letters the centre is always in the same place. Symmetries for the ear and the eye. But there is more.

The number of words in the entire passage is sixty-one, which divides by extreme and mean ratio at 38 and 23. As the thirty-eighth word from the beginning and the twenty-third word from the end are αυτωι ζωη, the golden section falls at 'in Him life'. The number of syllables is ninety-nine, which divides by extreme and mean ratio at 61 and 38. (Note the sequence: 23+38=61; 38+61=99.) The sixty-first syllable from the beginning and the thirty-eighth syllable from the end are in αυτωι. The number of letters is 219, which divides by extreme and mean ratio at 135 and 84. The 135th letter from the beginning and the eighty-fourth letter from the end are the upsilon and tau of αυτωι.

2 This conforms with the teaching of the *Rhetorica ad Herennium* IV XX 27–8 that one should compose either in actual equality, in which the numbers should be absolutely equal, or in apparent equality, in which the numbers may be approximately equal, admitting an imbalance of one or two. See Howlett, *Celtic Latin Tradition*, pp. 23–9, and *British Books in Biblical Style*, pp. 24–30.

This is only the Prologue to the Gospel. The very next sentence, chapter I verse 6, reads, 'There was a man sent from God whose name was John. He came for testimony, to bear witness to the light.' The chiastic pair to this is chapter XXI verse 24, 'This is the disciple who is bearing witness to these things and who has written these things, and we know that his testimony is true.' The former passage refers to John the Baptist, and the latter alludes to John the Evangelist, whose name is thus built into the fabric of the work without being explicitly mentioned.

In Jerome's Vulgate translation of the Prologue, there are nineteen words in A, arranged, nine, one, nine; thirty-seven syllables, arranged eighteen, one, eighteen; eighty-three letters, arranged forty-one, two, forty. In B there are eleven words, arranged five, one, five; nineteen syllables, arranged nine, one, nine; forty-six letters, arranged twenty-two, two, twenty-two. In C there are twelve words arranged eight, four. There are twenty syllables, arranged twelve, eight. The golden section of 20 falls at 12 and 8. There are forty-seven letters, arranged twenty-nine, eighteen. The golden section of 47 falls at 29 and 18. In D there are five words in the first clause and five in the second. There are eight syllables in the first clause and twelve in the second, the golden section of 20 falling at 12 and 8. There are twenty letters in the first clause and thirty-one in the second, the golden section of 51 falling at 31.5 and 19.5.

God is mentioned three times (3 x 1). The first example *Deum* is the ninth word (3 x 3). From the first *Deum* to the second *Deus* inclusive there are three words (3 x 1). From the second *Deus* to the third *Deum* inclusive there are nine words (3 x 3). After that there are thirty-three words (3 x 11) to the end of the Prologue. The verb *facere* appears three times, first as *facta*, the fourth word (4 x 1) of part B. Between the first *facta* and the second *factum* there are four words. After *factum* the fourth word is *factum*, after which there are twenty words (4 x 5) to the end of the Prologue. The fourth word after *factum* is *uita*. From *uita* to *uita* inclusive there are four words. From *lux* to *lux* inclusive there are four words. From *tenebris* to *tenebrae* inclusive there are four words, and *tenebrae* is the fourth word from the end of the Prologue.

Our author suggests in the first two words where he learned to compose like this. The only other text in the Bible which begins with those words is Genesis I 1. This unmistakeable allusion implies further that our author believes what he is telling us to be comparable in import with the Creation. If we bear in mind a passage from the beginning of Boethius *De Institutione Arithmetica* I II, *De Substantia Numeri*, '*Omnia quaecunque a primaeua rerum natura constructa sunt, numerorum uidentur ratione formata. Hoc enim fuit principale in animo Conditoris exemplar*', we might, as the Revd Professor Abbott Conway suggests, paraphrase John's Prologue 'In the beginning was proportion, and the proportion was with God, and God was the proportion; the same was in the beginning with God. All things through it came into being, and without it came into being not one thing. What came into being through it was life, and that life was the enlightenment of men. And the enlightenment in the darkness shines, and the darkness has not comprehended it.'

In the first part the twelve words in each half suggest twelve tribes and twelve apostles, the combined twenty-four words the elders of the Apocalypse. The number of syllables, 16+1+16, suggests the age of Jesus, 33. The number of letters, 37+3 suggests the number of days in the wilderness after baptism, 3+37 suggests the number of days from the Resurrection to the Ascension.

In the second part, about Christ's Creation of the universe, the ten words suggest ten commandments. The twenty-two syllables suggest the number of things God created in Genesis I, the number of generations from Adam to Israel, the number of letters in the Hebrew alphabet, and the number of books in the Hebrew Bible. The forty-six letters suggest the forty-six words in the account of the perfection of Sabbath rest in Genesis II 1–4, and the number of years it took, according to John II 20, to build the Temple.

From these four paradigms and other well known passages we infer ten rules of Biblical style.

1 A statement may be followed by a restatement in identical order, parallelism, as Isaiah I 10.
2 A statement may be followed by a restatement in reverse order, chiasmus, as Lamentations I 1.
3 Parallelism and chiasmus may be combined, as ai aii bi bii, b'i b'ii a'i a'ii, or exhibited simultaneously, the same passage making both patterns abcd d'c'b'a' and *abcd a'b'c'd'*, as Amos II 14–6.
4 The words of parallel members may be wholly or partly identical or synonymous, as Saint John's Gospel.
5 The nouns of parallel phrases may belong to the same declension and the verbs to the same conjugation, or nouns, adjectives, adverbs, and verbs in one may share the same roots as those in the other, as Genesis II 1–4.
6 A key word in one member may appear in the same position as its pair in the parallel, as Isaiah and Lamentations, or the first word of one member may be echoed by the last word of its parallel, as Amos.
7 Parallel phrases or clauses may be syntactically similar, as all four examples above.
8 Parallel members may be linked by puns or word play or by quotations from or allusions to other texts, as Saint Mark's Gospel and Saint John's Gospel.
9 Parallel members may be linked by alliteration, assonance, or rhyme.
10 Ideas stated at the beginning and the end of the first part of a passage or at the beginning and the centre of a passage may be restated together at the end, as Saint John's Gospel.

These are ten fundamental rules of composition in Biblical style. There are more, probably many more, but these may guide our inquiry for the present. They are all verbal devices which order the statement and restatement of ideas. But other sorts of device, which we may call adjuncts of Biblical style, govern other aspects of composition and presentation of texts.

II. ADJUNCTS OF BIBLICAL STYLE

There are five adjuncts, which we may consider as optional elements of Biblical style.[3] The first, second, and third, and the most pervasive, are cerebral, composition in mathematically determined forms. The fourth is aural, composition in rhythmical formulas. The fifth is visual, decoration of texts for the eye.

Concerning the first adjunct, arithmetical composition, Jews and Greeks alike believed that Creation itself had been a mathematical act, as described in the cosmogonies of Job XXXVIII 4–7, Isaiah XL 12, Proverbs VIII 22–31, and Sapientia XI 20, as well as Plato's *Timaeus* §§ 31–2, 35–6, and 41, read in the West in the Latin translation by Calcidius. The ratios by which God was believed to have created the universe are discussed explicitly by Plato, by Euclid in *Elements* Book II proposition xi and Book VI proposition xxx, and by Boethius *De Institutione Arithmetica* II LII and *De Instutitione Musica* I X. They are illustrated in Boethius's finest poem, *O qui perpetua mundum ratione gubernas*, placed at the symmetrical centre of *De Consolatione Philosophiae*. They include symmetry 1:1, *duplus* or duple ratio 2:1, the golden section or extreme and mean ratio, 0.61803 and 0.38197, *hemiolus* or sesquialter ratio 1½:1 or 3:2, *epitritus* or sesquitertian ratio 1⅓:1 or 4:3, *epogdous* or sesquioctave ratio 1⅛:1 or 9:8, or reckoned another way 1/9 and 8/9. There is explicit reference to the counting of verses, words, and letters of the text of the Hebrew Bible in the Talmud.[4] The units which writers counted include letters, syllables, words, metrical feet, lines of verse, clauses and phrases of prose, chapters, and entire books.

The second adjunct is, like the first, arithmetical. An author may place an important word or several important words at intervals in a text. There are three ways of reckoning this feature: first, counting from the first occurrence of the word to the second occurrence inclusively; second, counting between the occurrences of the word exclusively; third, including the first occurrence and excluding the second or excluding the first and including the second. There are conspicuous examples of all three ways of counting in passages from the Books of Judges and Genesis and the *Rhetorica ad Herennium* and *Cicero De Oratore*. We shall use specific locutions to distinguish the different forms of reckoning.

The third adjunct is also arithmetical. In Hebrew, as in Greek, every letter of the alphabet has a numerical value, unlike Latin, in which only seven letters, MDCLXVI, normally represent numbers. In Hebrew, by gematria, גימטריא, perhaps borrowed from γεωμετρια, a word or name may bear numerical value as well as semantic meaning. The name Caleb, כלב, has a numerical value of 20+30+2 or 52. So in Greek the name *Adam*, ΑΔΑΜ, has a numerical value of 1+4+1+40 or 46, and the name *Maria*, ΜΑΡΙΑ, 40+1+100+10+1 or 152, and the name *Jesus*, ΙΗϹΟΥϹ, 10+8+200+70+400+200 or 888, in Roman numerals

3 For fuller discussion and references see Howlett, *Celtic Latin Tradition*, pp. 1–54, and *British Books in Biblical Style*, pp. 1–100.

4 *Kiddushin* ch. I 30a–b, transl. Rabbi Dr H. Freedman in *The Babylonian Talmud: Seder Nashim*, ed. Rabbi Dr I. Epstein (London: Soncino Press, 1936), vol. VIII pp. 144–6.

DCCCLXXXVIII. In Latin *Diclux*, one of the names of Antichrist, who 'says' he is the 'light', exhibits this feature, the numerical value of the name being, like the number of the beast, 666 or DCLXVI. There is another widespread tradition of reckoning Latin letters as numerals, in which $A = 1, B = 2, C = 3, \ldots X = 20, Y = 21, Z = 22$, later after the adoption of $K = 10, X = 21, Y = 22, Z = 23$.

The fourth adjunct of Biblical style is rhythm. Greek writers from Thrasymachus in the fifth century B.C. and Classical Latin writers from the first century B.C. onward composed rhythmical prose. The tradition of composing clausulae, first in quantitative rhythms, then in mixed quantitative and stressed rhythms, and later in stressed rhythms only, evolved throughout the Late Latin period into the early Middle Ages.[5]

Although the subject of Latin prose rhythm is complicated and hotly debated, few scholars would deny the validity of a scheme of four basic rhythms with two variant forms.[6]

1	cretic + trochee or spondee	– ⏑ – – x	*forma uerborum*
2	double cretic	– ⏑ – – ⏑ x	*arte determinat*
3	cretic + double trochee or trochee + spondee	– ⏑ – – – ⏑ – x	*nuptias conparabat*
4	cretic + iambus	– ⏑ – ⏑ x	*ante diximus*
5	resolved cretic + trochee or spondee	– ⏑ ⏑ ⏑ – x	*esse puerile*
6	resolved cretic + cretic	– ⏑ ⏑ ⏑ – ⏑ x	*esse pueriliter*

The fifth and sixth forms are simply variants of the first and second in which the last long syllable of the cretic is resolved into two short syllables. In all forms the first cretic may be strengthened to a molossus (– – –). In all forms the last syllable is common, and the long syllables of the cretic may be resolved. The third form appears sometimes only as a trochaic metron without the cretic.

5 From an immense literature see Albert C. Clark, *The Cursus in Mediaeval and Vulgar Latin* (Oxford: Clarendon Press, 1910). S.F. Bonner, 'Roman Oratory', *Fifty Years (and Twelve) of Classical Scholarship* (Oxford: Basil Blackwell, 1968), pp. 416–64, esp. 439–40. *M. Tulli Ciceronis in L. Calpurnium Pisonem Oratio*, ed. R.G.M. Nisbet (Oxford: Clarendon Press, 1961), pp. xvii–xx. W.H. Shewring and K.J. Dover, 'Prose Rhythm', *The Oxford Classical Dictionary*, ed. N.G.L. Hammond and H.H. Scullard ed. 2 (Oxford: Clarendon Press, 1970), pp. 888–90. Tore Janson, *Prose Rhythm in Medieval Latin from the 9th to the 13th Century, Acta Universitatis Stockholmiensis, Studia Latina Stockholmiensia* XX (Stockholm: Almqvist and Wiksell International, 1975). R. Nisbet, 'Cola and Clausulae in Cicero's Speeches', *'Owls to Athens', Essays on Classical Subjects Presented to Sir Kenneth Dover*, ed. E.M. Craik (Oxford: Clarendon Press, 1990), pp. 349–59.

6 For illustration of these forms in the prose of the *Rhetorica ad Herennium* and Cicero *De Oratore* see Howlett, *Celtic Latin Tradition*, pp. 23–9, and *British Books in Biblical Style*, pp. 24–30. For maintenance of the tradition in Latin literary and epigraphic texts from the fifth century to the eleventh see Howlett, *Cambro-Latin Compositions*, pp. 6–15, 18–26, 39–42, 113–16.

The form of the cursus widely taught in the Middle Ages as part of the *ars dictaminis* required stressed rhythms which can be perceived as reflexes of these quantitative rhythms.

1	planus	/ x x / x	*tráctibus trúdit*
2	tardus	/ x x / x x	*fídens pernícibus*
3	uelox	/ x x \ x / x	*agmínibus cìrcumsaéptus*
4	medius	/ x / x x	*exercére stúdeat*
5	trispondiacus	/ x x x / x	*iaculórum catapúltas*
6	dispondeus dactylicus	/ x x x / x x	*felíciter perfrúitur*

The fifth adjunct is the disposition of capital letters and punctuation marks in texts, not merely for decorative and syntactical purposes, but for articulation of structural features of Biblical style.

These rules and adjuncts of Biblical style are widely exhibited in Late Latin and early Mediaeval literatures, not confined exclusively to Insular cultures. But the style appears in both prose and verse, in both Latin and vernacular, beginning early and continuing in uninterrupted use by hundreds of writers who quote their predecessors and communicate with their contemporaries in easily demonstrable succession from the fifth century onward. In the chapters that follow we shall see clear evidence of a coherent tradition among Insular writers of diplomatic instruments from the seventh century to the fifteenth.

II

ENGLISH CHARTERS

THE OLDEST CHARTERS OF KENTISH KINGS

I. HLOTHHERE KING OF THE MEN OF KENT TO BEORHTWEALD ABBOT OF RECULVER

The oldest extant Anglo-Saxon charter with a sustainable claim to authenticity and integrity, extant in London, British Library, MS Cotton Augustus II.2, records in seventh-century English uncial script a grant of land in the Isle of Thanet and at Sturry in Kent from King Hlothhere to Abbot Beorhtweald and his monastery at Reculver, in the year 679.[1]

I + IN NOMINE DOMINI NOSTRI SALUATŎRĪS IHĒSŪ XPĪSTĪ .
EGO HLOTHARIUS REX CÁNTUĀRĬŎRUM
PRO REMEDIUM ANIMAE MEAE DONO TERRAM . IN TENID . QUAE
APPĒLLĀTŪR . UUĒSTĂN ∴ AĒ
TIBI BERCUALD . TUÓQUE MONASTÉRIO
CUM OMNIBUS AD SE PĒRTĬNĒNTĪBŪS
CAMPIS PASCUIS MARISCIS[a] SILUIS MODICIS . FONTĀNĪS[b] PĪSCĀRĬĪS[c]
OMNIBUS UT DICTUM EST AD EANDEM TERRAM PĒRTĬNĒNTĪBŪS[d] .
SICUTI NUNC ŬSQUĔ PŌSSĒSSA ĒST .
IUXTA NOTISSIMOS TERMINOS A ME DEMONSTRATOS[e] ET
PROACURATŎRĬBŪS MĔĪS .
II EODEM MODO TIBI TUOQUE MONASTÉRIO CONFÉRIMUS .
TENEAS POSSIDEAS[f] TU . POSTERIQUE TUI IN PERPÉTUŪM DĒFĒNDĀNT
III A NULLŌ CŎNTRĀDĪCĀTŬR[g] .

1 P.H. Sawyer, *Anglo-Saxon Charters, An Annotated List and Bibliography*, Royal Historical Society Guides and Handbooks VIII (London: Royal Historical Society, 1968), no. 8 p. 72. W. de Gray Birch, *Cartularium Saxonicum*, 3 vols (London: Whiting and Company and Charles J. Clarke, 1885–93), no. 45 vol. I pp. 70–1. *Facsimiles of Ancient Charters in the British Museum* (London: British Museum, 1873), pl. 1. E.A. Lowe, *English Uncial* (Oxford: Clarendon Press, 1960), pl. xxi. *Chartae Latinae Antiquiores, Facsimile-Edition of the Latin Charters Prior to the Ninth Century*, ed. A. Bruckner and R. Marichal, Part III British Museum London (Olten and Lausanne: Urs Graf-Verlag, 1963), no. 182 pp. 20–1. Pierre Chaplais, 'Some Early Anglo-Saxon Diplomas on Single Sheets: Originals or Copies?', in *Prisca Munimenta*, ed. Felicity Ranger (London: University of London Press, 1973), pp. 63–87. Leslie Webster and Janet

IIII CUM CONSENSU ARCHIEPISCOPI THEODORI ET ĘDRICI[h] . FÍLII[i] FRATRIS MEI

NECNON ET OMNIUM PRINCIPUM .

SICUTI TIBI DONATA EST ITA TENE ET POSTERI TUI :—

V QUISQUIS CONTRA HANC DONATIONEM UENÍRE TEMPTAUERIT

SIT AB OMNI XPISTIANITÁTE[j] SEPARATUS .

ET A CORPORE ET SANGUINE[k] DOMINI NOSTRI IHESU XPISTI SUSPENSUS .

MANENTEM HANC DONATIONIS CHARTULAM IN SUA NIHILOMINUS . FIRMITATE

VI ET PRO CONFIRMATIONE EIUS MANU PROPRIA SIGNUM SANCTAE . CRÚCIS EXPRÉSSI[l]

VII ET TESTES UT SUBSCRÍBERENT ROGAUI .

VIII ACTUM IN CÍUITATE RECUULF .

IN MENSE MAIO INDICTIONE SEPTIMA :—

VIIII IN IPSA ANTE MEMORATO DIE ADIUNXI ALIAM TERRAM IN STURIA

IUXTA NOTISSIMOS TERMINOS A ME DEMONSTRATOS[e] ET PROACURATORIBUS MEIS

CUM CAMPIS ET SILUIS ET PRATIS

SICUTI ANTE MEMORAUIMUS[m] SUPRA DICTAM TERRAM .

X ITA ISTA SIT A ME DONATA EODEM MODO CUM OMNIBUS AD SE PERTINENTIBUS[n]

IN POTESTATE ABBATIS SIT . IN PERPETUUM . A ME DONATA .

XI A NULLO CONTRADICATUR[g] QUOD ABSIT :

NEQUE A ME NEQUE A PARENTIBUS MEIS NEQUE AB ALIIS .

XII SI ALIQUIS ALITER FECERIT A DEO SE DAMNATUM SCIAT .

ET IN DIE IUDICII RATIONEM REDDET DEO IN ANIMA SUA :—

I + SIGNUM MANUS HLOTHARI RÉGIS DONATÓRIS [.]
II + SIGNUM MANUS GUMBERCTI :
III + SIGNUM MANUS GĘBREDI :—
IIII + SIGNUM MANUS OSFRIDI :—
V + SIGNUM MANUS IRMINREDI [:]
VI + SIGNUM MANUS AEDILMAERI .
VII + SIGNUM MANUS HAGANI .
VIII + SIGNUM MANUS AELDREDI :
VIIII + SIGNUM MANUS ALDHODI :—
X + SIGNUM MANUS GUDHARDI :
XI + SIGNUM MANUS BERNHARDI .
XII + SIGNUM MANUS UELHISCI :.—:.—

a MERISCIS. b FON / NIS. c PISCARIS. d PERTINENTIA. e DEMONSTRATUS. f POSSEDEAS. g CONTRADICITUR. h ĘDRICO. i FILIUM. j XPIANI / TATA. k SANGUINI. l EXPRAESSI. m MEMORABIMUS. n PERTINEN / TINENTIA *with erasure of the former* NEN / TI.

Backhouse ed., *The Making of England, Anglo-Saxon Art and Culture* A.D. *600–900* (London: British Museum and British Library, 1991), no. 27.

I + In the name of the Lord, Our Saviour, Jesus Christ,
I, Hlothhere, King of the men dwelling in Kent,
for the cure of my soul give land in 'Thanet' which is called 'West of the Stream'
to you, Beorhtweald, and to your monastery,
with all things pertaining to it,
fields, pastures, marshes, little woods, springs [or 'wells'], fish ponds,
all things, as has been said, pertaining to the same land,
just as it has been possessed until now,
according to the very well known bounds designated by me and my procurators [or 'stewards'].
II In the same manner we collate [it] to you and your monastery;
may you hold [and] possess and your successors defend [it] in perpetuity.
III Let it be contradicted by no man.
IIII With the consent of Archbishop Theodore and of Eadric the son of my brother
and also of all leading men;
just as it has been given to you so hold, and your successors.
V Whoever may attempt to come against this donation,
may he be separated from all the Christian community
and suspended from the body and blood of Our Lord Jesus Christ,
this little charter of donation remaining nonetheless in its own effect [or 'validity'].
VI And for its confirmation I have impressed with my own hand the sign of the holy cross.
VII And I have asked witnesses that they subscribe [lit. 'write below'].
VIII Executed in the city of 'Reculver'
in the month of May in the seventh indiction.
VIIII In the same [indiction] on the day called to mind before I adjoined other land in Sturry
according to the very well known bounds designated by me and my procurators [or 'stewards'],
with fields and woods and meadows,
just as we have called to mind before concerning the said land.
X As this may be given by me in the same manner with all things pertaining to it
let it be in the power of the abbot in perpetuity, given by me.
XI Let it be contradicted by no man, which God forbid,
neither by me nor by my relations nor by others.
XII If anyone should do otherwise he should know himself damned by God
and on the day of judgement he will give back an account to God in his own soul.

I + Sign of the hand of Hlothhere the king, the giver.
II + Sign of the hand of Gumbeorht.
III + Sign of the hand of Giefræd.
IIII + Sign of the hand of Osfrith.
V + Sign of the hand of Eormenræd.
VI + Sign of the hand of Æthelmær.
VII + Sign of the hand of Hagan.
VIII + Sign of the hand of Ealdræd.
VIIII + Sign of the hand of Ealdhod.

X + Sign of the hand of Guthheard.
XI + Sign of the hand of Beornheard.
XII + Sign of the hand of Wilhyse.

The text of the charter divides into nine parts fixed by chiastic statement and restatement of words and ideas. The charter begins in lines 1–2, in which the ninth word names the king, '*ego Hlotharius* | *rex Cantuariorum*.

The second part is lines 3–10:

A dono
B tibi Bercuald tuoque monasterio
C1 cum omnibus ad se pertinentibus
C2 campis pascuis mariscis siluis modicis fontanis piscariis
C1' omnibus ut dictum est ad eandem terram pertinentibus
D sicuti nunc usque possessa est
C' eodem modo
B' tibi tuoque monasterio
A' conferimus.

The writer refers to the act of granting in A and A', to the recipients in B and B', the particulars of the grant in C and C', and to possession at the crux in D. Note the nine locutions *omnibus, campis, pascuis, mariscis, siluis modicis, fontanis, piscariis, omnibus, eodem modo*.

The third part is lines 11–15:

A teneas … tu posterique tui
B a nullo
C archiepiscopi Theodori
D et
C' Ędrici filii fratris mei
B' necnon et omnium principum
A' tene et posteri tui.

The writer refers to holding and posterity in A and A', to a possible objector and actual supporters in B and B', to named supporters in C and C'. Among the thirty-one words from *tu posterique tui* to *posteri tui* inclusive, referring to Beorhtweald's successors, the central sixteenth word is *Ędrici* | *filii* | *fratris mei*, referring to Hlothhere's successor.

The fourth part is lines 16–19:

A hanc donationem
B sit ab omni Xpistianitate separatus
C et
B' a corpore et sanguine Domini nostri Ihesu Xpisti suspensus
A' hanc donationis chartulam.

The writer refers to this donation in A and A' and to excommunication in B and B'.

The fifth part is lines 20–3:

A et ... expressi
A' et ... rogaui
A in ciuitate Recuulf
A' in mense Maio.

The sixth part is lines 24–7:

A ante memorato die
B cum campis et siluis et pratis
A' ante memorauimus.

The seventh part is lines 28–9:

A a me donata
B eodem modo
C cum omnibus ad se pertinentibus
C' in potestate abbatis sit
B' in perpetuum
A' a me donata.

The eighth part is lines 30–1:

A a nullo contradicatur
B quod absit
A' neque a me neque a parentibus meis neque ab aliis.

The ninth part is lines 32–3:

A si aliquis aliter fecerit a Deo se damnatum sciat
B et
A' in die iudicii rationem reddet Deo in anima sua.

There are in A and A' two parallel lines of nine words each, in which the sixth of each is *Deo*.

Let us note next that these nine discrete sections are bound by more comprehensive chiastic and parallel links:

A1 In nomine Domini nostri Saluatoris Ihesu Xpisti
A2 ego Hlotharius rex Cantuariorum
A3 dono
B1 terram in Tened
B2 cum
B3 campis
B4 siluis
B5 ut dictum est
B6 ad eandam terram
B7 pertinentibus
B8 in perpetuum
B9 a nullo contradicatur
B10 quisquis contra hanc donationem uenire temptauerit
B11 sit ab omni Xpistianitate separatus
C indictione septima
C' in ipsa
B'1 aliam terram in Sturia
B'2 cum
B'3 campis
B'4 siluis
B'5 sicuti ante memorauimus
B'6 supra dictam terram
B'7 pertinentibus
B'8 in perpetuum
B'9 a nullo contradicatur
B'10 si aliquis aliter fecerit
B'11 a Deo se damnatum sciat
A'1 in die iudicii rationem reddet Deo in anima sua
A'2 Signum manus Hlothari regis
A'3 donatoris.

Let us note further that the third sentence contains three words. Two identical clauses do not participate in the structures considered above, *iuxta notissimos terminos a me demonstratos et proacuratoribus meis*. The former is the ninth line from the beginning of the charter; the latter is in the ninth sentence and in the ninth line from the end of the charter; both lines contain nine words.

Let us note next the ratios of music theory by which ancient and mediaeval men believed that God had created the universe: symmetry (1:1), *duplus* or duple ratio (2:1), the golden section or extreme and mean ratio (0.61803 and 0.38197), *hemiolus* or sesquialter ratio ($1\frac{1}{2}:1$ or 3:2), *epitritus* or sesquitertian ratio ($1\frac{1}{3}:1$ or 4:3), and *epogdous* or sesquioctave ratio (reckoned one way $1\frac{1}{8}:1$ or 9:8 and another way $\frac{1}{9}$ and $\frac{8}{9}$).

The charter contains 240 words, which divide by symmetry at 120 and 120. The text of the charter begins *In nomine Domini nostri Saluatoris Ihesu Xpisti* 1. The 120th word is the last of *Domini nostri Ihesu Xpisti* 18. Before the nine-word clause in the ninth line from the beginning there are fifty-two words, and after the nine-word clause in the ninth line from the end there are sixty-eight words, together 120.

The charter of twelve sentences is attested by twelve witnesses. The charter of 240 words is concluded by an attestation of 242 letters.[2]

The 240 words of the charter divide by duple ratio at 160 and 80, at the title of the man who may have composed it, | *archiepiscopi Theodori* 13.[3] The first eighty words divide by the same ratio at 53 and 27, at a reference to the recipient, *tibi Bercuald tuoque monasterio* | 4. The last 160 words divide by the same ratio at 107 and 53, at a reference to the donor, | *a me donata* 28. From *dono* 3 to *donata est* 15 inclusive there are eighty words. Between *hanc donationis chartulam* | 19 and | *donata* 29 there are eighty words.

The 240 words divide by extreme and mean ratio at 148 and 92, at a reference to the recipient of the charter, | *tibi donata est* 15, and at the reference to the place and time of donation, *in ciuitate Recuulf* | *in mense Maio* 22–3. The first ninety-two words divide by the same ratio at 57 and 35, at a reference to the donor, *a me* | 9. The last 148 words divide by the same ratio at 91 and 57, at a reference to the donation, *dictam* | *terram* 27.

The 240 words divide by sesquialter ratio at 144 and 96, at the king's request to the witnesses at the centre of the central fifth part of the charter, *et testes ut subscriberent rogaui* | 21. The ninety-sixth word of the charter is the last of *sicuti tibi donata est ita* 15. From the first word of that phrase to the last of *sicuti ... ita ista sit* 27–8 there are also ninety-six words. The first ninety-six words divide by symmetry at *sicuti* 8, the forty-eighth word of the charter.

The 240 words divide by sesquitertian ratio at 137 and 103, at the king's reference to his own signing of the charter, *manu propria signum sanctae* | *crucis expressi* 20.

Observing a widespread convention the composer of this charter referred at one-ninth and eight-ninths of the text to the recipients and the donor. The 240 words divide by one-ninth and eight-ninths at 27 and 213, at *tibi Bercuald tuoque monasterio* | 4 and *neque a* | *me* 31.

The charter begins with a reference to Jesus Christ, Whose ministry began when He was thirty years old. From the beginning to the first mention of the

2 For allowance in apparent equality of a margin of one or two see above p. 7 n. 2.

3 The acts of the Synod of Hertford recorded by Bede in *Historia Ecclesiastica* IV v, *Quam sententiam definitionis nostrae Titillo notario scribendam dictaui* [*sc. Theodorus*], might imply either that Theodore dictated the text verbatim to a copyist who merely wrote it down or that he reported the gist to a notary who composed the text. The illiterate Wihtræd, on the other hand, is unlikely to have dictated the charter to Eabbe considered below, pp. 37–9. For the petition Wilfrid submitted to a Roman synod to protest the diminution of his authority see Howlett, 'Insular Latin Writers' Rhythms', pp. 88–92. Theodore and Hadrian were not the only men capable of such composition, and Canterbury was not the only centre in which men practised such composition.

name, in *in nomine domini nostri saluatóris* | *Ihesu*, there are thirty letters. Jesus lived on earth for thirty-three years and had twelve disciples. The charter occupies thirty-three lines of prose followed by twelve signs manual, after which even the punctuation marks may be arranged chiastically: [.] : :— :— [:] . and . : :— : . .

Preservation of the Classical diphthong *ae* in *animae suae* … *quae* 3 and *sanctae* 20 (later flattened to *e*) is consistent with the orthography of works known to have issued from the school of Theodore and Hadrian from A.D. 670 onward.[4] Separation of the words *in perpetuum* 11 and 29 and *supra dictam* 27 and lack of assimilation in *in perpetuum*, not *imperpetuum*, and the spelling *nihilominus* 19, not *nichilominus*, are consistent with features of other late-seventh-century texts from the school of Theodore and Hadrian.[5] The orthography of the king's name, *Hlotharius* 2, is identical with that in Bede, *Historia Ecclesiastica* IV XVII [XV]. The spellings *mariscis* 6, *demonstratos* 9 and 25, *possideas* 11, *contradicatur* 12 and 30, *Ędrici filii* 13, *Xpistianitate* 17, *sanguine* 18, *expressi* 20, and *memorauimus* 27 are required for orthography, grammar, and syntax. The manuscript reading *fonnis* 6 may have issued from loss of the syllable *-ta-* between *fon-* at the end of one line in the manuscript and *-nis* at the beginning of the next.[6] The spelling *piscariis* 6 for the manuscript reading *piscaris* is etymologically correct, and it conforms with the rhythm of a molossus—cretic. The spelling *pertinentibus* 7 and 28 is required for grammar and syntax and consistency with *pertinentibus* 5. The spelling *proacuratoribus* 9 and 25 may be explained as the preposition *a*, parallel with that in *a me* 9 and 25, in tmesis in *procuratoribus*.[7] Further justifications for correction will be considered below.[8]

The accusative absolute in *manentem hanc donationis chartulam* 18 may be compared with the nominative and genitive absolutes in Theodore's *Laterculus Malalianus*.[9] The title in the phrase *cum consensu archiepiscopi Theodori* 13 is also consistent with the date of the charter. Pope Vitalian sent Theodore to England as Bishop of Canterbury, the title with which he signed synodical instruments, as at Hertford, 24 September 672, *ego quidem Theodorus quamuis indignus ab apostolica sede destinatus Doruuernensis ecclesiae episcopus*.[10] Pope Agatho may have awarded the title of metropolitan archbishop as late as 678, giving Theodore

4 Howlett, 'Aldhelm and Irish Learning', pp. 37–75, '*Aldhelmi Carmen Rhythmicum*', pp. 119–40, *British Books in Biblical Style*, pp. 102–28, and 'Insular Latin Writers' Rhythms', pp. 92–8.

5 Jane Stevenson, *The 'Laterculus Malalianus' and the School of Archbishop Theodore*, Cambridge Studies in Anglo-Saxon England XIV (Cambridge University Press, 1995). *Biblical Commentaries from the Canterbury School of Theodore and Hadrian*, ed. Bernhard Bischoff and Michael Lapidge, Cambridge Studies in Anglo-Saxon England X (Cambridge University Press, 1994).

6 Chaplais, 'Diplomas', p. 66.

7 I owe this suggestion to Leofranc Holford-Strevens.

8 See pp. 25–6.

9 *Laterculus Malalianus*, ch. XI p. 134.

10 Bede, *Historia Ecclesiastica* IV V.

authority to divide the dioceses of other bishops, notably Wilfrid.[11] At the Synod of Hatfield, 17 September 679, Theodore presided [*imperante*] *Hlothario rege Cantuariorum regni eius anno septimo praesidente Theodoro gratia Dei archiepiscopo Brittanniae insulae et ciuitatis Doruuernis.*[12]

In the widely attested convention of using letters of the alphabet as numbers, *A* = 1, *B* = 2, *C* = 3, ... *X* = 20, *Y* = 21, *Z* = 22, the name *BERCUALD* bears a numerical value of 2+5+12+3+19+1+10+4 or 56. From the beginning of the charter to *tibi* | *Bercuald* there are fifty-six syllables.

The text of the charter contains 574 syllables and the signatures of the witnesses ninety-two syllables. Reckoning one syllable, for *crux,* for the initial cross and the twelve crosses before the witnesses' signatures, we find 1+574+92+12 or 679, a confirmation, perhaps, of the year of the grant.[13]

By the most critical reckoning there are nineteen erroneous letters in this text, in sixteen places, with three of the mistakes made twice. None is serious; some by the standards of the time might not be errors;[14] all are simple slips of spelling such as even a competent scribe might make in an almost, if not exactly, contemporary fair copy of an original document. At worst, the rate of error in this document is 0.011, though if some of the forms are not erroneous the rate might be 0.008. More important evidence is the syntactical correctness of the prose. But most important evidence for the original integral and authentic state of the text of this charter is the correctness of the clausular rhythms. That is what establishes the ambitious literary register of the composition, the rhythms of which are consistent with those in extant works of Theodore, notably letters and the *Laterculus Malalianus.*[15] Of the thirty-three lines of text thirty exhibit faultless clausular rhythms. One might wrench clausular rhythms on to the remaining three lines by inferring false quantities in *tuoque monasterio* 4, in which the closed syllable with the etymologically short vowel *a* should be long by position, followed by the consonant *t*, and in *monasterio conferimus* 10, in which the second syllable of *conferimus* is normally short, and in *crucis expressi* 20, in which the first syllable of *crucis* is normally short. But *tuóque monastério* 4 and *monastério conférimus* 10 exhibit the acceptable cursus rhythm *dispondeus dactylicus*, and *crúcis*

11 The intention may have been to make English dioceses small enough for a bishop to perambulate during a year, more like small Mediterranean dioceses based upon the city and small Irish dioceses based upon the *tuath*, less like the immense territories governed by Wilfrid. For analysis of the petition Wilfrid submitted to protest diminution of his authority see above p. 19 n. 3.

12 Bede, *Historia Ecclesiastica* IV XVII [XV].

13 For evidence that the Welsh and the Irish reckoned by the Dominical Incarnation from the sixth and seventh centuries onward, long before Bede is usually supposed to have made the system popular, see Howlett, *Celtic Latin Tradition*, pp. 91–102, 138–52, 187–93, and *Cambro-Latin Compositions*, pp. 42–3, 67–8.

14 *possedeas, contradicitur, sanguini, memorabimus.*

15 Howlett, 'Insular Latin Writers' Rhythms', pp. 92–3, 95–6.

expréssi 20 exhibits the acceptable rhythm *cursus planus*. We will observe below reasons for considering these features neither erroneous nor inconsistent, but deliberate. Meanwhile there are many reasons to admire the competent craftsmanship and, some may think, beauty of this oldest extant English charter.

II. EADRIC KING OF THE MEN OF KENT TO SAINT PETER'S IN CANTERBURY

Here follows the text of another early Anglo-Saxon charter with a sustainable claim to authenticity and integrity, recording a grant of three sulungs of land near Stodmarsh in Kent from King Eadric to the monastery of Saint Peter in Canterbury in June 686.[16] It survives in two copies, both from Saint Augustine's, Canterbury, one thirteenth-century, London, British Library, MS Cotton Julius D.II, folio 131r (F), and the other fifteenth-century, Cambridge, Trinity Hall, MS 1, folios 52v–53r (N). The text, with capital letters and punctuation marks in boldface, represents the Cotton manuscript.

I **IN** nomine saluatoris cuius pietate regimen ádsecuti[a] sú*mus* a
quo etiam gubernánte regná*mus* a
et omnia quae habere cognoscimur ipso largiente hábita pòssidé*mus* **.** a
II **Pr**o qua re ego Eadricus rex Cántuariórum b
a praesente die et tempore térram iuris mé*i* c
quamuis pretium cónpetens[b] accéperi*m*[c] b
hoc est argénti libras déc*em* **.** b
in monasterio beati Petri apostolórum príncip*is* d
quod situm est iuxta ciuitátem Dòrouérn*is* d
una cum consensu meorum patriciorum in perpetuum donáui̧ et dón*o* e
III **Q**uae supra dicta terra coniuncta est terrae quam sanctae memóriae Hlothárius[d] d
quondam rex beato Petro pro remedio animae suae donásse cognósci*tur* **.** f
IIII **Q**uae térra detérminá*tur* **.** f
V **E**x una parte habet uadum quod appellatur Ford strata[e] pública indiréct*um* b
et a parte alia flumen quod nóminátur S*tur* **.** f
VI **O**mnes terras sationales **.** cum pratis **.** campis **.** síluis **.** fontáni*s* d
uel mariscum quód appellátur Stód Mer*sc*[f] **.** g
cum omnibus ad supra dictam terram aratrorum trium pértinéntibu*s*[g] d
beato Petro eiusque familiae in qua nunc praeesse Hadrianus[h] abbas dinoscitur trádidi pòssidénda*s*[i] d
VII **E**t quicquid exinde fácere uolúerin*t* h
utpote domini liberam hábeant pòtestát*em* b

16 Sawyer, *Charters*, no. 9 pp. 72–3. *Charters of St Augustine's Abbey Canterbury and Minster-in-Thanet*, ed. S.E. Kelly, Anglo-Saxon Charters IV (Oxford University Press for the British Academy, 1995), no. 7 pp. 30–1.

VIII Sicut donatum est manére decérn*o* e
nunquam me heredesque meos uel successores contra hanc donatiónis meae chártul*am*[j] b
ullo tempore ésse uentúro*s* . d
VIIII Quod si áliquis praesúmpseri*t* : h
sit separatus a participatione corporis et sanguinis Domini nóstri Ihesu Xpíst*i* . c
manente hac chartula[k] nihilominus[l] in súa firmitát*e* . j
X De quibus omnibus supra dictis ac a mé definíti*s* d
ut ne aliqua[m] in posterum sít aduérsita*s* . d
propria manu signum sanctae crúcis expréss*i* : c
XI Et sanctissimum atque reuerentissimum Theodorum archiepíscopum nóstr*um* b
ut subscriberet rogaui . et alios téstes simílite*r* . f
XII Actum in mense Iunio indictione[n] .xiiii. [i.e. quártadécima]

+[o] Ego Eadricus[p] rex in hanc donationis meae chartulam[j] signum sanctae crúcis expréssi[q] .
+ Ego Theodorus archiepiscopus gratia Déi subscrípsi .

By analogy with the preceding charter I have for manuscript spellings in e *silently restored* ae *where it is etymologically correct.* a F assecuti. b conpetentem. c F acciperim. d F Clotharius N Lotharius. e F streta. f F Stodmerse. g FN pertinentia. h FN adrianus. i F possidendam. j F cartulam. k F cartula. l FN nichilominus. m FN aliquis. n F inditione. o F *omits* +. p FN Ædricus. q F *ends here.*

I In the name of the Saviour in reverence for Whom we have succeeded to rule, with Whom governing also we rule,
and all things which we are known to have we possess with the Same bestowing the things had.
II For which reason I, Eadric, King of the men dwelling in Kent,
from the present day and time
though I have received a suitable price,
this is ten pounds of silver,
in the monastery of blessed Peter prince of the apostles,
which is sited next to the city of Canterbury,
together with the consent of my noble men have given and give in perpetuity land of my right.
III Which above said land is conjoined to the land which King Hlothhere of holy memory
is known to have given formerly to blessed Peter for the cure of his own soul.
IIII Which land is bounded.
V On one side it has the ford which is called 'Ford' not in a straight line from the public road
and on the other side the river which is named 'Stour'.
VI All arable lands with meadows, fields, woods, springs [or 'wells']
or the marsh that is called 'Stud Marsh'

with all things pertaining to the above said land of three ploughlands
to blessed Peter and to his family, in which Hadrian the abbot is known to be preeminent now, I have handed over to be possessed.
VII And whatever thereafter they may wish to do
they should, say, have the free power of a lord.
VIII Just as it has been given I declare [it] to remain,
I and my heirs or successors to be bound never to come against this little charter of my donation
at any time.
VIIII Which, if anyone should presume,
let him be separated from having a part of the body and blood of Our Lord Jesus Christ,
this little charter remaining nonetheless in its effect [or 'validity'].
X Concerning all which things above said and determined by me
lest there be any adversity at a later time
with my own hand I have impressed the sign of the holy cross.
XI And I have asked the most holy and most reverend Theodore our archbishop
that he subscribe [lit. 'write below'] and other witnesses similarly.
XII Executed in the month of June in the fourteenth indiction.

+ I, Eadric, King, have impressed the sign of the holy cross on to this little charter of my donation.
+ I, Theodore, Archbishop by the grace of God, have subscribed [lit. 'written below'].

Like the charter of A.D. 679 from Hlothhere to the monastery at Reculver this charter of A.D. 686 from Eadric to the monastery of Saint Peter at Canterbury contains thirty-three lines and 240 words. The lines of this charter exhibit rhyme, the first three aaa, then in groups of four, of which three rhyme, bcbb, dded, ffbf, dgdd. The Romano-Briton Faustus of Riez, fourth son of Vortigern, composed comprehensively rhyming rhythmical prose during the fifth century,[17] and Irishmen composed rhyming rhythmical prose from the end of the sixth century onward,[18] but this is the earliest example yet known of Anglo-Latin rhyming rhythmical prose.

Also like the charter of A.D. 679 this charter contains twelve sentences. The first sentence of the attestation contains twelve words.

The 240 words divide by duple ratio at 160 and 80, at *Hlotharius quondam rex* | 12. The first eighty words divide again by duple ratio at 53 and 27, at *ego Eadricus rex* | 4.

The words divide by extreme and mean ratio at 148 and 92. From | *in monasterio beati Petri* 8 to *beato Petro eiusque familiae* | 19 inclusive there are

17 Howlett, *Cambro-Latin Compositions*, pp. 6–15.
18 Howlett, 'Insular Latin Writers' Rhythms', pp. 58–67.

ninety-two words. Those ninety-two words divide again by extreme and mean ratio at 57 and 35. From | *beati Petri* 8 to *beato Petro* | 12 inclusive there are thirty-five words. From | *eiusque familiae in qua nunc praeesse Hadrianus abbas dinoscitur* 19 to *sanctissimum et reuerentissimum Theodorum archiepiscopum nostrum* | 31 inclusive there are ninety-two words.

The words divide by sesquialter ratio at 144 and 96. From | *terram* 5 to *terram* | 18 inclusive there are ninety-six words. Those ninety-six words divide again by sesquialter ratio at 58 and 38. From | *terram* 5 to *supra dicta terra* | 11 inclusive there are thirty-eight words. From | *terram* 5 to *quae terra determinatur* | 13 inclusive there are fifty-eight words. From | *quae terra determinatur* 13 to | *ad supra dictam terram* 18 there are thirty-eight words. The thirty-eight words divide again by sesquialter ratio at 23 and 15. From | *terra* 13 to *terras* | 16 inclusive there are twenty-three words.

The words divide by one-ninth and eight-ninths at 27 and 213, at *ego Eadricus rex* | *Cantuariorum* 4.

Note the passage from | *terram iuris mei* 5 to *argenti libras decem* | 7 inclusive. In that first reference to the land involved and the price paid for it, ten pounds, there are between *terram* and *decem* ten words.

Reckoning letters as numerals the name *PETRUS* bears a numerical value of 14+5+18+16+19+17 or 89. From | *monasterio beati Petri* 8 to *beato Petro* | 12 inclusive there are eighty-nine syllables. From | *monasterio beati Petri* 8 to *beato Petro* | 19 inclusive there are eighty-nine words.

As these charters of Hlothhere and Eadric exhibit so many identical features, the orthography of each may corroborate that of the other. Because of consistent spellings in *ae* in the former I have silently restored *ae* for manuscript *e* in the latter. In the latter after correcting the manuscript reading *possidendam* 19, agreeing with the false antecedent *terram* 18, to *possidendas*, agreeing with the correct antecedents *omnes terras* 17 and *cum omnibus ... pertinentibus* 18, the final *s* in *possidendas* rhyming with final *s* in *fontanis* 16 and *pertinentibus* 18, and comparing this with *possidemus* 3, one confirms the correctness of *possideas* 11 in the former charter, corrupted to *possedeas* perhaps by a scribe with his eye on the first vowel of the preceding word *teneas* 11 or the second of *possessa* 8. In the latter charter long *e* in *acceperim* 6, not *acciperim*, is required both for grammar and for the rhythm of the molossus. In the latter charter correct Latin *mariscum* and correct Old English *mersc* 17 both justify correction in the former charter to *mariscis* 6 and suggest that interference from the vernacular form produced the misspelling *meriscis*. Correct spelling of *chartulam* 19 in the seventh-century copy of the former charter justifies restoration of *h* to *chartulam* 23 and 34 and *chartula* 27 in the thirteenth-century copy of the latter charter. Similarly correct spelling of *nihilominus* 19 in the former justifies removal of *c* from *nihilominus* 27 in the latter. The correct spelling *expressi* 30 and 34 in the latter justifies correction to *expressi* 20 in the former. The unassimilated form *in perpetuum* 11 and 29 in the former agrees with the unassimilated forms *conpetens* 6, *in perpetuum* 10, *nunquam* 23, and *in posterum* 29 in the latter. Separation of the words *in perpetuum* 11 and

29 and *supra dictam* 27 in the former justifies separation of *in perpetuum* 10, *supra dictam* 18, and *in posterum* 29 in the latter. Only if these locutions are separated do the charters exhibit the same number of words.

As in Hlothhere's charter, of the thirty-three lines of text thirty exhibit quantitative rhythms. Line 9 ends with the quantitative verse rhythm of a dactylic hexameter and the acceptable rhythm of the *cursus planus*. Line 30 ends also with a *cursus planus*. Line 32 ends with the rhythm of the *cursus tardus* and line 33 with the rhythm of the *cursus medius*.

Dr Kelly considers that 'the structure of the dispositive section itself is rather muddled, in part because the draftsman has included awkward details about the location of the estate, as well as a primitive boundary clause'.[19] Recognition of the structural principles by which the draftsman composed rescues him from any charge of muddle or awkwardness, revealing instead his competent craftsmanship.

III. A REVISED CHARTER OF HLOTHHERE TO SAINT PETER'S IN CANTERBURY

Another charter records a grant of three sulungs of land in Stodmarsh near Fordwich in Kent, from King Hlothhere to the abbot and monastery of Saint Peter in Canterbury, on 1 April 675.[20] It survives in a fifteenth-century copy, Cambridge, Trinity Hall, MS 1, folio 52r–v.

In nomine Domini Dei et Saluatóris Ihesu Xpísti.
ego Lotharius rex Cántuariórum
anno regni nostri primo indiccióne tércia
sub die kalendárum Aprílis
cum concilio uenerabilis archiepíscopi Thèodóri
atque consensu primórum meórum
terram trium aratrorum in marisco qui appellatur Stodmerch' iúxta Fordeuuícum
cum pratis campis siluis fontanis paludibus fluminibus et omnibus ad eandem pertinéntibus rébus
in ipsa quantitate sicut antiquitus predecessores mei reges predicta líbere tènuérunt
abbati et monasterio beati Petri apostolórum príncipis
quod situm est iuxta ciuitatem Dorouernis ín subúrbio
in sempiterno possidenda concedimus ét confirmámus
ita ut nec nobis nec aliquibus successórum nostrórum
regum siue principum aut ecclesiasticarum dignitátum grádibus
nefario temeritatis ausu aliquando infringere uel diminuere aliquid de donacione nóstra líceat
sed pro remedio anime mee et absolucione peccatórum meórum

19 Kelly, *Charters*, p. 31.
20 Sawyer, no. 7. Birch, no. 36. Kelly, no. 6 pp. 26–7.

ita ut predixi famulis Dei absque aliqua lesione omnia predicta in euum stabília permáneant .
II Quisque autem heredum successorumque meorum regum Cancie
uel si quilibet secularium dignitatum aut etiam ecclesiasticarum de supradicta donacione
quam pro eterna remuneracione anime mee omnipotenti Deo ad utilitatem famuláncium
ei in ius monasteriale constat esse largitam[a]
aliquid disrumpere aut immutare uel irritum facere tentáuerit
sciat se sine dubio omnipotenti Deo fraudem facere
et proinde coram eo et sanctis angelis eius eterno anathémate réum .
III Quicunque uero hec que largita prediximus sub pia proteccione cústodíerit
uel Dei intuitu misericórditer aúxerit
sit benedictus in secula
audiatque in die nouissimo tremendi examinis
ab ipso Iudice omnium Xpisto Domino eterne benediccionis uocem
'Venite benedicti Patris mei percipite regnum quod uobis paratum est ab origine mundi'
manente igitur hac cartula in sua semper firmitate
cum religiosis testibus signo dominice crucis in hoc loco qui dícitur Dorouernis
stabiliter in euum confirmamus .

I + Ego Lotharius rex Cancie suprascripta signo sancte crucis per propriam mánum roboráui .
II + Ego Theodorus gracia Dei archiepiscopus rogatus a rége subscrípsi .
III + Ego Adrianus abbas indígnus subscrípsi .
IIII + Sígnum manus Écca .
V + Sígnum Ósfridi .

a largitum.

I In the name of the Lord God and Saviour Jesus Christ,
I, Hlothhere, King of the men dwelling in Kent,
in the first year of our reign in the third indiction,
on the day of the kalends of April,
with the counsel of the venerable archbishop Theodore
and the consent of my leading men,
land of three ploughlands in the marsh which is called 'Studmarsh' next to 'Fordwich',
with the meadows, fields, woods, springs [or 'wells'], swamps, rivers, and all things pertaining to the same [land]
in the very quantity just as of old my predecessors, kings, held the foresaid things freely,
to the abbot and monastery of blessed Peter, prince of the apostles,

which is sited next to the city of Canterbury in a suburb
we concede and confirm to be possessed for eternity,
so that neither to us nor to any of our successors,
in grades of kings or princes or ecclesiastical dignities
should it be permitted by nefarious daring of temerity at any time to infringe or diminish anything from our donation,
but for the cure of my soul and absolution of my sins,
so that, as I have said before, all the foresaid things without any harm should remain for the servants of God stable for an age.

II For whoever of my heirs and successors of the kings of Kent,
or if anyone of secular or even ecclesiastical dignities from the abovesaid donation,
which for an eternal remuneration for my soul for the use of those serving omnipotent God
is fitting to be bestowed for Him into monastic right,
should attempt to disrupt or change or nullify anything,
let him know himself without doubt to commit fraud to omnipotent God
and therefore before Him and His holy angels guilty by eternal anathema.

III But whoever would under holy protection guard these bestowed things which we have foresaid
or increase mercifully under the gaze of God,
may he be blessed for ages,
and may he hear on the last day of the tremendous judgement
from the very Judge of all, Christ the Lord, the voice of eternal blessing,
'Come, you blessed ones of My Father, receive the kingdom which has been prepared for you from the beginning of the world',
with this little charter remaining always therefore in its own effect [or 'validity']
with religious witnesses by the sign of the Dominical cross in this place which is called Canterbury
stably for an age we confirm.

I + I, Hlothhere, King of Kent, have corroborated the things written above by the sign of the holy cross through my own hand.
II + I, Theodore, by the grace of God archbishop, asked by the king, have subscribed.
III + I, Hadrian, unworthy abbot, have subscribed.
IIII + Sign of the hand of Ecca.
V + Sign of Osfrith.

Although this charter survives only in a fifteenth-century copy, the thirteenth-century historian Thomas Sprott may have seen an earlier copy.[21] Some features imply that this text is based upon an early and authentic document, not least the recording of a gift mentioned in Eadric's charter as an earlier donation, and the fact of composition in thirty-three lines. If this were completely authentic it

21 Kelly, *Charters*, p. 29.

would be a witness to the text of the oldest extant English charter. But there are grounds for suspicion.

First, the chronology is inconsistent. The charter 'is dated 1 April, in Hlothhere's first year as king and in the third indiction. The indiction points to 674–5, but the regnal year is problematic, because it seems to suggest that Hlothhere's reign began rather later than the date given by Bede for his succession.'[22] We have seen above that the acts of the Synod of Hatfield describe the year 679 as [*imperante*] *Hlothario rege Cantuariorum regni eius anno septimo*. After the acts of the Synod of Hertford in *Historia Ecclesiastica* IV V Bede wrote *facta est autem haec synodus anno ab incarnatione Domini* †DCCLXX*tertio* [*sic* Colgrave and Mynors. *lege* DCLXX *tertio*, an error for *secundo*], *quo anno rex Cantuariorum Ecgberct mense Iulio obierat, succedente in regnum fratre Hlothere*.

Second, a seventh-century Anglo-Saxon king is unlikely to have used a territorial title like *rex Cancie* 18, as distinct from an ethnic title like *rex Cantuariorum* 2.

Third, no one has yet adduced evidence that Theodore received or used the title of archbishop before 678 or 679.

Fourth, the phrase *archiepiscopi Theodori* 5 does not conform with any acceptable clausular rhythm; nor do lines 9, 14, 15, 17, 20, 22, 24, 25, and 26 exhibit the quantitative rhythms we have observed above in genuine charters. One line, 32, ends with the verse rhythm of a dactylic hexameter. If one assumed that the rhythmic basis of this charter was not quantitative but stressed, it would be difficult to account for line 29. A noteworthy 36% of the lines of this charter lack good clausular rhythms, and line 29 lacks even cursus rhythm.

Fifth, the spelling has not been reproduced exactly from an early authentic document. No one in the seventh century would have written *Stodmerch'* or *Fordeuuicum* 7. The flattening of the Classical diphthong *ae* to *e* and assimilation of *inmutare* and *inritum* to *immutare* and *irritum* 22, and the replacement of *t* by *c* in *Cancie* 18, *donacione* 19, *remuneracione* 20 are all signs of later revision. So is the spelling of *concilio* 5 for *consilio*, unlikely from an Anglo-Saxon who pronounced *c* as *k*, but likely from a later Francophone who pronounced *c* before *e* or *i* as *s*.

Sixth, the number of words is nowhere near 240.

Seventh, the number of sentences is nowhere near twelve, and there is no obvious correlation between numbers of any elements in the charter proper and in the attestation.

Finally, there is no object for the concluding verb.

Dr Kelly considers 'the assumption that early Kentish charters would necessarily follow a fairly strict pattern' to be 'certainly debatable'.[23] But the first two texts analysed above show that they were tightly composed in fixed forms specifically to guard against the sort of alteration that the third text underwent.

We may accept Hlothhere's charter of 679 and Eadric's charter of 686 as integral and authentic texts which have been transmitted to us nearly in their

22 *Ibid.*, p. 27.
23 *Ibid.*, p. 28.

original forms. We may accept Hlothhere's charter of 675 as based, perhaps, on an integral and authentic document, but transmitted to us in revised form.[24] We may for new reasons consider what have long been reckoned outright forgeries, the charters purporting to have issued from King Æthelbeorht, Bishop Augustine, and King Eadbald to the monastery of Saints Peter and Paul, Canterbury, at the beginning of the seventh century. These forgeries, numbered 2, 3, 4, 1244, 6 by Sawyer, 4, 5, 6, 7, 13 by Birch, and 1, 2, 3, 4, 5 by Kelly, derive from the first generation after the Conquest. They were written by men unfamiliar with the tradition of composition we have been considering, a tradition that had been practised and transmitted for centuries in these islands in hopes of revealing, if not of frustrating, the efforts of those who would either tamper with genuine old texts or forge new texts that pretended to antiquity.[25] The monuments of this tradition can be recovered in minute particulars. To discover whether the system still works let us test it on other charters.

THE OLDEST CHARTERS OF MINSTER-IN-THANET

IIII. SWÆFHEARD KING OF THE MEN OF KENT TO EABBE ABBESS OF MINSTER-IN-THANET

Here follows the text of a charter from the period about A.D. 690 from Swæfheard King of the men of Kent to Abbess Eabbe, preserved in London, British Library, MS Cotton Julius D. II, folio 102r.[26]

24 The extent of revision may be determined by scholars more competent than the present writer in diplomatic.

25 For clear examples of failure by another early Norman to understand the informing principles of earlier Insular compositions see David Howlett, 'Symeon's Structural Style: Experiments in Deconstruction' in *Symeon of Durham Historian of Durham and the North*, ed. David Rollason, Studies in North-Eastern History I (Stamford: Shaun Tyas, 1998), pp. 254–81. For evidence that Normans came to terms with this tradition of composition see Howlett, *The English Origins of Old French Literature*; 'A Polyglot Glossary of the Twelfth Century' in *De Mot en Mot: Aspects of Medieval Linguistics; Essays in Honour of William Rothwell*, ed. Stewart Gregory and D.A. Trotter (Cardiff: University of Wales Press and Modern Humanities Research Association, 1997), pp 81–91; 'Artful Anglo-Norman Prose: The Structure of *De Plaiz de Corone*', *Romania* (forthcoming).

26 Sawyer, no. 11. Birch, no. 41. Kelly, no. 41 pp. 146–7.

I **IN** nomine Saluatoris **E**go Suabertus rex Cántuari*orum* a
miserationum Domini memor quas erga mé exércu*it* . b
II **I**deo ego[a] réctum iudicá*ui* . c
ut pro aeterna salute animae meae atque me*órum* . a
aliquid munusculum Dómino inpénd*erem*[b] . a
III **I**d est[c] terram quae sita est in Sturige .ii. [i.e. duórum] aratr*órum* a
atque .iii. aratrorum in loco qui[d] dícitur Bótdesha*m* a
monasteriali potestati atque regulariter uiuéntibus subíc*erem* . a
Quod hodierna die Domino auxiliánte conplé*ui*[e] . c
Dedique uenerabili abbatissae Eabbae[f] ut ibi seruientium Deo préces protelé*ntur* d
atque pro uita mea sine defectu in conspectu Déi effúndá*ntur* . d
IIII **E**t ad confirmationem donatiónis istíus . e
signum sanctae crúcis expréss*i* . c
V **N**ecnon et principes meos ut similiter fácerent rogá*ui* . c
VI **S**ícque fécérun*t* . b
ut si aliquis ausu nefariae temeritatis aliquid ex ea auferre uel minúere uolúer*it* : b
nouerit se alienatum a Deo in resurrectióne iust*órum* . a

+ Signum Suaberti **R**egis .

In this and the following three charters I have for manuscript spellings in e *silently restored* ae *and* oe *where they are etymologically correct.* a & b impenderem. c idem. d que. e compleui. f Rabe.

I In the name of the Saviour I, Swæfheard, King of the men dwelling in Kent,
[am] mindful of the mercies of the Lord which He has performed for me.
II Therefore I have judged it right
that for the eternal salvation of my soul and my people's
I should devote [lit. 'weigh out'] some little gift for the Lord.
III That is, land which is sited in 'Sturry', of two ploughlands,
and of three ploughlands in the place which is called 'Boda's Ham',
I should subject to monastic authority and to those living according to rule,
which on today's day I have completed with the Lord helping,
and have given to the venerable Abbess Eabbe so that the prayers of those serving God there might be driven forth
and be poured out for my life without cessation in the sight of God.
IIII And for confirmation of this donation
I have impressed the sign of the holy cross.
V And I have asked my leading men also that they do similarly.
VI And so they have done,
so that if anyone by an attempt of nefarious temerity should wish to take away or diminish anything from it
he should know himself alienated from God in the resurrection of just men.

+ Sign of Swæfheard the King.

Words and ideas have been arranged in chiastic and parallel patterns:

A Suabertus rex
B miserationum Domini memor quas erga me exercuit
C1 iudicaui
C2 ut
C3 pro aeterna salute animae meae
C4 meorum
C5 aliquid
D Domino
E inpendere
F in Sturige
G ii aratrorum
H atque
G' iii aratrorum
F' in loco qui dicitur Botdesham
E' subicerem
D' Domino
C'1 conpleui
C'2 ut
C'3 pro uita mea
C'4 meos
C'5 aliquid
B' nouerit se alienatum a Deo in resurrectione iustorum
A' Suaberti regis.

If we reckon the shortest full line to contain four words, this charter is exactly half as long as the two genuine charters considered above, six sentences and sixteen and one-half lines and 120 words. As in them, all the lines of this charter but three end with correct clausular rhythms. Line 4 ends with a hexameter verse rhythm, line 8 with a cursus rhythm *dispondeus dactylicus*, and line 13 with a *cursus planus*.

Reckoning letters as numerals the palindromic name *EABBAE* bears a numerical value of 5+1+2+2+1+5 or 16. The charter to Eabba contains sixteen full lines, and the half-line *sicque fecerunt.*, which occurs after line 14, contains fourteen letters, one space between words, and one punctuation point, together sixteen.

V. OSWINE KING OF THE MEN OF KENT TO EABBE ABBESS OF MINSTER-IN-THANET

Here follows another charter, dated 27 January 690, from Oswine King of the men of Kent to Abbess Eabbe, from the same source, folio 102r.[27]

27 Sawyer, no. 13. Birch, no. 35. Kelly, no. 42 pp. 149–50.

I [+] **IN** nomine Domini Ihesu Xpisti Saluatór*is* . a
Ego Osuuinus rex Cántuarió*rum* b
aliquod munusculum pro Deo destino dar*e* c
ut sit refrigerium animae meae ín perpétu*um* . b
et uigilet mea memoria cum sánctis in sublim*e* . c
II **A**nno secúndo regni me*i* . d
indictione autem tertia sub die .vi. kalendarum . Fébruari*i* . d
pro remedio animae mea*e* . c
et absolutione peccatorum meorum ecclesiastico iur*e* c
concedo quandam terram que dicitur Stúrig*e*[a] c
id est decem manentes ex e*a* e
cum siluis et campis ac palúd*ibus* . a
cum fluminibus ac font*ibus* . a
cum pratis ac pomariis[b] et cum omnibus útensíl*ibus* a
in ipsa quantitate sicut principes a regibus antiquitus per donátum possedér*unt* . f
almae[c] Eábbae[d] abbat*issae* . c
atque carnali propinquitate prox*imae* . c
in Deoque matri monasteriali iuri dono perpétuo trád*o* : g
quatinus habeat possideatque proprio arb*itrio* . g
III **E**t cuicumque uoluerit uiuens uel morien*s* a
habeat integram facultatem condonare . tantum ín domín*io*[e] . g
IIII **I**stud autem territorium a me módo conmemor*átum*[f] b
ac pro Déo per don*átum* b
in praesentia principum meorum qui ad praésens haberi poss*unt* . f
hoc est Cantuariorum quos iure ac propria nostra potestate ádipísci*mur* . h
pro testimonio confirmationis ad subscri*béndum* b
ac ad cónsent*iéndum* b
mihi huic donationi conduxi in hunc locum qui dícitur Dorouern*is* . a
V **C**onfirmamus stabíliter in a*éuum* b
ut quisquis hanc donationem meam mente maliuola disrúmpere temptáu*erit* . f
sciat se coram Deo et sanctis angelis eius aeterno anathémate r*éum* . b
VI **Q**uisquis uero bene addendo custod*ierit* : f
sit benedictus in saecul*a* . e

I [+] **T**heodorus gratia Dei archiepiscopus rogatus a rége subscrípsi .
II + **E**go Osuuinus propria manu subscrípsi ac conséusi .
III [+ Ego Suebhardus conséusi et subscrípsi .
IIII + Ego Hadrianus abbas indígnus subscrípsi .
V + Sígnum manus Écca .
VI + Sígnum Ósfridi .]

a sturrie. b pomeriis. c aliene. d aebbe. e domino. f commemoratum.

I In the name of the Lord Jesus Christ, the Saviour
I, Oswine, King of the men dwelling in Kent,
intend to give a certain little gift for God
so that there might be relief for my soul in perpetuity
and that memory of me may remain watchful among the saints in the height.
II In the second year of my reign
in, moreover, the third indiction, on the sixth day of the kalends of February
for the cure of my soul
and absolution of my sins by ecclesiastical right
I concede certain land which is called 'Sturry',
that is, ten hides from it,
with woods and fields and swamps,
with rivers and springs [or 'wells'],
with meadows and orchards and with all useful things,
in the very quantity, just as leading men possessed it by way of donation from kings of old,
to Eabbe the holy abbess
and one very close in fleshly relationship
and a mother in God I hand over to monastic right in a perpetual gift,
so that she may have and possess according to her own judgement.
III And to whomever she may wish, living or dying,
she may have a complete faculty to grant, as far as the right of lordship.
IIII But this territory called to mind by me now
and by way of donation for God
in the presence of my leading men who can be had at present,
this is of the men dwelling in Kent whom we have received by inheritance by law and by our own power,
for subscribing as witness of confirmation
and for consenting
I have for myself led together to this place which is called Canterbury for this donation.
V We confirm stably for an age
that whoever would attempt with a malevolent mind to disrupt this my donation
should know himself before God and His holy angels guilty by eternal anathema.
VI But whoever would guard [it] well by adding
should be blessed for ages.

I + Theodore by the grace of God archbishop, asked by the king, I have subscribed.
II + I, Oswine, with my own hand have subscribed and consented.
III + I, Swæfheard, have consented and subscribed.
IIII + I, Hadrian, unworthy abbot, have subscribed.
V + Sign of the hand of Ecca.
VI + Sign of Osfrid.

Let us note first some infixed features of discrete passages. In the second sentence the second word is *secundo*. In the second line of this sentence the third word is *tertia*, and the sixth word is *.vi.* As the date, *sub die .vi. kalendarum Februarii*, is 27 January, there are twenty-seven letters before | *vi kalendarum*

Februarii. There are ten lines of text before the detail of the grant, *id est decem manentes*, in which the tenth letter is the last of *decem*. In line 16 the words *Eabbae abbatissae* contain sixteen letters. From the beginning of the charter to *uiuens* | 20 inclusive there are exactly 690 letters, coincident with the year of the grant.

Let us note next features that guarantee the structure of the entire composition. The text of the charter contains six sentences, and it is attested by six witnesses. The text of the charter contains thirty-three lines. Including the preliminary cross and the signatures of the witnesses there are 240 words.

VI. OSWINE KING OF THE MEN OF KENT TO EABBE ABBESS OF MINSTER-IN-THANET

Here follows another charter from the period about A.D. 690 from Oswine to Eabbe, from the same source, folio 102r–v.[28]

I **IN** nomine Domini nóstri Ihesu Xpísti .
Ego Osuuinus rex Cántuariórum .
gratias refero miserenti Déo omnipoténti
qui confirmauit me in regno pátrum meórum .
et dedit mihi domum cognátionis meae .
II **Q**uam ob rem placuit mihi ne ingratus beneficiis Dómini uidérer :
et terram quae sita est in insula Tenet .xviii. manéntes continéntem
quam aliquando Irminrédus possidébat
et aliqua pars ipsius archiepíscopi érat .
ipso támen consèntiénte
et aliam a nóbis accipiénte .
monasteriali seruitúti subiéci .
III **N**uncque in praesentia adiuuante Domino perpetraui sub manus Xpísticolárum
gubernatrici Eabbae[a] perpetuali donatióne redégi :
ut teneat . possideat ipsa semper successoresque eius incommutabili decréto
défendant
atque ad confirmationem ístius chártulae[b] :
caespitem terrae supra dictae sacro altari súper pósui
ut omnis quicumque ausus fuerit aliquid ex ea temerare aút minúere
uel etiam transmutare . sine uoluntate póssidéntium :
sciat se alienum a participatione regni ecclésiis éffici
et a coetu fidélium sègregátum :
nisi regulariter émendáuerit .

[+] **S**ignum sanctae crucis propria mánu expréssi .
I [+] Signum manus Ósuuini régis .
II + Ego Suebhardus consénsi et subscrípsi .
III + Sígnum manus Áccae.

a eabe. b cartule.

28 Sawyer, no. 14. Birch, no. 40. Kelly, no. 43 p. 152.

I In the name of Our Lord Jesus Christ
I, Oswine, King of the men dwelling in Kent,
give back thanks to merciful omnipotent God,
Who has confirmed me in the realm of my fathers
and given to me the house of my kinsfolk.
II On which account it has pleased me, lest I be seen ungrateful for the benefits of the Lord,
that the land which also is sited in the island 'Thanet' containing eighteen hides,
which Eormenræd used formerly to possess,
and another part of it was the archbishop's,
he, however, consenting,
and receiving another from us,
I have subjected to monastic service.
III And now in [his] presence, with the Lord helping, I have brought it about under the hands of worshippers of Christ,
I have brought it to the governess Eabbe in perpetual donation,
that she may hold, may possess, she always, and her successors may defend [it] with incommutable resolve,
and for confirmation of this little charter
I have placed on the holy altar a turf of the above said land,
so that every and each who might dare to violate or diminish anything from it
or even to change without the will of those possessing
should know himself to be made alien from participation in the churches of the realm
and separated from the throng of faithful men
unless he would amend according to rule.

\+ The sign of the holy cross I have impressed with my own hand.
I + Sign of the hand of Oswine the King.
II + I, Swæfheard, have consented and subscribed.
III + Sign of the hand of Acca.

In sentence II there are eighteen words before *.xviii.*

The charter contains two-thirds of thirty-three, twenty-two lines, the number of things God created in Genesis I 1 – II 4, the number of letters in the Hebrew alphabet, the number of books in the Hebrew Bible, the number of syllables in the account of Christ's creation of the universe in the Greek text of John I. The charter contains from the beginning to *expressi* inclusive 144 words, the number of cubits in the wall of the heavenly Jerusalem (Apocalypse XXI 12) and part of the number of the elect (Apocalypse VII 4).

The text of the charter consists of three sentences, and it is attested by three witnesses. Three of the lines do not exhibit clausular rhythms. Lines 3, 11, and 14 end with the cadence of a hexameter verse.

VII. WIHTRÆD KING OF THE MEN OF KENT TO EABBE ABBESS OF MINSTER-IN-THANET

Here follows a fourth charter, dated 17 July 694, from King Wihtræd to Abbess Eabbe, from the same source, folio 102v.[29]

I **IN** nomine Domini Déi Saluatóris
Ego Uuihtredus rex Cantuariorum[a] una cum coniuge mea Kinigitha regina .
referens gratias . Largitori bonórum Dómino .
qui dilatauit terminos nostros iuxta patérnam antiquitátem .
in commune pertractauimus aliquam partem terrae nobis conlatae ad uícem repéndere
ne ingrati beneficiis uideremur Lárgitoris nóstri .
II **Q**ua de re . a praesenti die et témpore
tibi religiosae Eabbae[b] abbatissae[c] Deoque dicátae féminae .
terram iuris nostri quae sita est in ínsula Téneti .
quae quondam appellata est Humantun[d] aratrorum .iiii. [i.e. quáttuor] contúlimus .
in perpétuum possidéndam .
ut cum omnibus ad eandem pértinéntibus .
pratis campis . fontanis siluis piscáriis flumínibus .
marisco et quicquid ad supra dictam térram pértinet
[a .iiii. partibus orientis occidentis . aquilonis et meridiei .]
tuo usui ditioníque[e] subícias .
III Teneas[f] possideas . dones . cómmutes . uénundes .
uel quicquid exinde fácere uolúeris :
liberam hábeas potestátem .
IIII Successoresque tui defendant ín perpétuum .
Nunquam me heredesque meos contra hanc chartulam[g] descriptionis nostrae aliquando ésse uentúros .
V **A**d cuius cumulum etiam áffirmatiónis .
caespitem huius supra dictae terrae super sanctum altáre pósui .
VI Et propria manu pro ignorantia litterarum signum sanctae crucis in hac chártula[h] expréssi .
VII Sed[i] et Kinigítha[j] idípsum fécit .
VIII **P**rincipesque meos ut pari modo propriis manibus fácerent rogáui .
quorum nomina súbtus adnécta[k] sunt .
VIIII **S**i quis[l] quod absit : contra hanc chartulam[m] a me factam uel heredes mei contra íre praesúmpserint :
nouerint se[n] a participatione corporis et sanguinis Domini nostri Ihesu Xpisti ésse aliénos

29 Sawyer, no. 15. Birch, no. 86. Kelly, no. 44 p. 154.

et a coetu fidélium ségregándos .
híc et in aetérnum .
X Quam saepe dictam chartulam[g] scribéndam dictáui
XI Et tibi Eabbae[o] abbatissae trádidi cónseruándam .
XII **A**ctum .xvi. kalendas Augusti . indictione .vii. anno regni nóstri tértio .

[+ Signum manus Uuihtredi regis .
+ Signum manus Kinigithae reginae .
+ Signum manus Bernhardi .
+ Signum manus Alhuuardi .]

a cantie. b eabbe. c abbatissie. d humantiun. e dicionique. f teneat. g cartulam. h kartula. i set. j kynygytha. k annecta. l quid. m kartulam. n MS *omits*. o eabe.

I In the name of the Lord God, the Saviour
I, Wihtræd, King of the men dwelling in Kent, together with my wife Cynegith the queen,
giving back thanks to the Lord, the Bestower of good things,
Who has spread out our bounds with respect to paternal antiquity,
have considered to give in return for the common good a certain piece of land given to us,
lest we be seen ungrateful for the benefits of our Bestower.
II On which account from the present day and time
to you, Eabbe, religious abbess and woman dedicated to God,
land of our right which is sited in the island of Thanet,
which once was called 'Huma's Tun', of four ploughlands, we have conferred
to be possessed in perpetuity,
so that with all things pertaining to the same,
meadows, fields, springs [or 'wells'], woods, fish ponds, rivers,
marsh, and whatever pertains to the above said land
[from the four parts of east, west, north, and south]
you may subject to your use and direction.
III You may hold, possess, give, change, sell,
or whatever you may wish to do thence
you should have free power.
IIII And may your successors defend [it] in perpetuity,
I and my heirs to be bound never to come against this little charter of our writing out at any time.
V Also for consummation of the affirming of which
I have placed a turf of this above said land on the holy altar.
VI And with my own hand, because of ignorance of letters I have impressed the sign of the holy cross on this little charter.
VIII But Cynegith has also done the same.
VIIII And I have asked my leading men that they do in like manner with their own hands,
whose names are adjoined below.
X If anyone, which God forbid, against this little charter made by me, even my heirs, should presume to go against,

they should know themselves to be alien from having a share of the body and
blood of Our Lord Jesus Christ,
and to be segregated from the throng of faithful men
here and for eternity.
XI Which oft-said charter I have dictated to be written
and I have handed over to you, Abbess Eabbe, to be conserved.
XII Executed on the sixteenth of the kalends of August in the seventh indiction
in the third year of our reign.

[+ Sign of the hand of Wihtræd the King.
+ Sign of the hand of Cynegith the Queen.
+ Sign of the hand of Beornheard.
+ Sign of the hand of Ealhweard.

In sentence II in the the fourth line there are after *.iiii.* four syllables to the end of the line. The attestation contains four signs manual.

Like other early genuine charters this composition contains twelve sentences. Inclusion of the phrase bracketed before line 15 would increase the number of lines in this text from the expected 33 to 34 and the number of words from the expected 240 to 248. The phrase recurs in only one other Anglo-Saxon charter,[30] and that of doubtful authenticity, supposedly from *Cenwulf rex una cum coniuge mea Cenegiða regina*, allegedly in the year 799, but recorded not earlier than the tenth century. Recurrence of the queens' names *Kinigitha* and *Cenegiða* is a noteworthy coincidence, perhaps not unrelated to the appearance of the bracketed phrase, that inclines one further toward scepticism about authenticity of the latter charter and about inclusion of the bracketed phrase in the original text of the former charter.

VIII. WIHTRÆD KING OF THE MEN OF KENT TO SAINT MARY'S IN LYMINGE

Here follows a charter of Wihtræd King of the men of Kent to the church of Saint Mary at Lyminge, in London, British Library, Stowe Charter 1, dated July 697, written in Insular half-uncial script of the late seventh or early eighth century.[31]

I + **IN** nomine Domini Dei nóstri Ihesu Xpísti
Ego Uihtredus rex Cántuariórum
prouidens mihi in futuro decreui dare aliquid omnia míhi donánti

30 Sawyer, no. 156. Birch, no. 296.

31 Sawyer, no. 19. Birch, no. 97. W. Basevi Sanders, *Facsimiles of Anglo-Saxon Manuscripts* (Southampton: Ordnance Survey, 1884), vol. III pl. 1. Pierre Chaplais, 'Who Introduced Charters into England? The Case for Augustine', in *Prisca Munimenta*, pp. 88–107 at 102–5.

II **E**t consílio accépto
bonum uisum est conferre basilicae[a] beatae Mariae génetricis Déi
quae sita est in loco qui dícitur Límingae .
terram .IIII. aratrorum quae dicitur Pleghelmes[b] . Tun .
cum omnibus ad eandem terram pertinentibus
iuxta notissimos terminos id est Bere Ueg . et Méguuines Paeð et Strét Leg .
III Quam donationem meam uolo firmam esse in perpetuum
ut nec ego seu heredes mei aliquid minúere praesúmant .
IIII **Q**uod si aliter temptatum fuerit a quálibet persona
sub anathematis interdictione sciat sé praeuaricari
V Ad cuius confirmationem pro ignorántia litterarum
+ signum sanctae crúcis expréssi
VI Et testes idoneos ut subscríberent rogáui
id est Berichtualdum árchiepíscopum uirum uénerábilem[c]

+ **E**go Berichtuualdus episcopus rogatus consensi et subscripsi[d] .
+ **S**ignum manus Uihtredi regis
+ **S**ignum manus Aethilburgae reginae
+ **S**ignum manus Enfridi .
+ **S**ignum manus Aedilfridi .
+ **S**ignum manus Hagana .
+ **S**ignum manus Botta .
+ **S**ignum manus Bernhaerdi .
+ **S**ignum manus Theabul .
+ **S**ignum manus Frodi
+ **S**ignum manus Aehcha
+ **S**ignum manus Aessica .
+ **S**ignum manus Adda .
+ **S**ignum manus Egisberichti

Actum in mense Iulio indictione xma

ðæs landes boc æt Berdhelhames ƿicum
boc nunc ƿigelmigne Tun .
ƿihtredus rex Ca.' ad ecclesiam de Limming .
ƿielmestun .iiij. aratrorum. Latine .
Wihtredus cepit regnare 693 et obiit 726 .

a bassilicae. b ƿieghelmes *with* ƿi *written over erasure.* c *The last two words have been added in a later hand.* d subscribsi.

I + In the name of the Lord Our God, Jesus Christ
I, Wihtræd, King of the men dwelling in Kent,
seeing ahead for myself in the future, have decided to give something to the One giving all things to me.
II And with counsel received,
it has seemed good to confer to the basilica of blessed Mary, begetter of God,

which is sited in the place which is called 'Lyminge',
land of four ploughlands which is called 'Pleghelm's Tun',
with all things pertaining to the same land,
according to the very well known bounds, that is 'Bere Way' and 'Megwine's Path' and 'Stret Ley'.
III This my donation I wish to be firm in perpetuity,
so that neither I nor my heirs should presume to diminish anything.
IIII If anything should be attempted otherwise by any person
he should know himself to transgress under an interdiction of anathema.
V For the confirmation of which, because of ignorance of letters,
+ I have impressed the sign of the holy cross.
VI And I have asked suitable witnesses that they subscribe,
this is, Beorhtweald the archbishop, a venerable man.

+ I Beorhtweald Bishop, asked, have consented and subscribed.
+ Sign of the hand of Wihtræd the King.
+ Sign of the hand of Æthelburh the Queen.
+ Sign of the hand of Eanfrith.
+ Sign of the hand of Æthelfrith.
+ Sign of the hand of Hagan.
+ Sign of the hand of Botta.
+ Sign of the hand of Beornheard.
+ Sign of the hand of Theabul.
+ Sign of the hand of Frod.
+ Sign of the hand of Aehcha.
+ Sign of the hand of Aessica.
+ Sign of the hand of Adda.
+ Sign of the hand of Egisbeorht.
Executed in the month of July in the tenth indiction.

In line 1 in the words *in nomine Domini Dei nostri Ihesu* there are thirty-three letters and spaces between words.

From the space before | *Ego Uihtredus rex Cantuariorum* 2 to | *beatae Mariae* 5 there are twenty-two words and 152 letters and spaces between words, the numerical value of the name MAPIA in Greek alpha-numeric notation being 40+1+100+10+1 or 152.

In sentence II the fourth line contains the description of four ploughlands. Line 7 contains seven words.

Like the charter of A.D. 679 from Hlothhere to Abbot Beorhtweald this exhibits the phrase *iuxta notissimos terminos* in the ninth line. Like the charter of about A.D. 690 from Swæfheard to Abbess Eabbe this contains six sentences and sixteen and one-half lines and 120 words, exactly half of the twelve sentences and thirty-three lines and 240 words we have noted in other integral and authentic charters.

VIIII. ANOTHER FORM OF THE SAME

Another form of this charter survives in London, British Library, MS Cotton Augustus II.88, from the year 700 or 715, written in Insular half-uncial of the early eighth century.[32] It exhibits only a few differences in spelling: *Uuihtredus* 2, *basilicae* and *Mariæ* 5, omission of *in* 10, *inminuere* 11, *Berhtuualdum* 17, and in the subscriptions *Berhtuualdus, rogat', subscripsi, Uuihtredi, Aesica,* and *xiiima.* Between lines 9 and 10 it includes a passage five lines and forty-four words long.

terrulae quoque partem eiusdem Dei genetrici beatae Mariae similiter in perpetuum possidéndam pérdono .
cuius uocabulum est Rúmining Séta .
ad pastum uidelicet óuium trècentórum .
Ad australem quippe fluminis quae appellatur Limina Ea .
Terminos uero huius terrulae . ideo non ponimus quoniam ab accolis úndique cérti sunt .

also part of the same little piece of land I give over to be possessed in perpetuity similarly to blessed Mary, begetter of God,
of which the name is 'Ruminining Seta',
for pasture, that is, of three hundred sheep,
to the south, namely, of the river which is called 'Limina River'.
The bounds, however, of this little land we do not put for the reason that they are definitely known on all sides by those who dwell there.

It also exhibits different endorsements.

Rumening seta inn to Limining mynster .
Wictredus rex Cantuarie contulit ecclesie sancte Marie de Limminge .iiii. aratra .
Plegelmestun et Rumingsete ad pastum ouium ccc .

32 Sawyer, no. 21. Birch, no. 98. *Ancient Charters*, pl. 4.

CHARTERS FROM ESSEX, MIDDLESEX, AND MERCIA

X. ÆTHELRÆD AN EAST SAXON LAYMAN TO ÆTHELBURH ABBESS OF BARKING

Here follows a text, extant in London, British Library, MS Cotton Augustus II.29 in seventh- or eighth-century English uncial script, that records a grant by a layman.[33]

I +**I**N NOMINE DOMINI NOSTRI IHESU XPISTI SALUATORIS .
QUOTIENS SANCTIS AC UENERABILIBUS LOCIS UESTRIS ALIQUID OFFERRE UIDEMUR .
UESTRA UOBIS REDDIMUS NON NOSTRA LARGIMUR .
II **Q**UAPROPTER EGO **H**ODILREDUS . PARENS SEBBI PROUINCIA EASTSEXANORUM .
CUM IPSIUS CONSENSU
PROPRIA UOLUNTATE SANA MENTE INTEGROQUE CONSILIO
TIBI HEDILBÚRGAE[a] ABBATISSAE
AD AUGMENTUM MONASTERII TUI QUAE DÍCITUR . BEDDAN HAAM .
III PERPETUALITER TRADO ET DE MEO IURE IN TUO TRANSSCRIBO TERRAM
QUAE APPELLATUR RICINGA HAAM BUDIN HAAM DECCAN HAAM ANGENLABES HAAM
ET CAMPO IN SILUA QUAE DÍCITUR UUIDMUNDES FELT
QUAE SIMUL SUNT CONIUNCTA .LXXU. [*i.e.* SEPTUAGINTA QUÍNQUE *altered to* .XL. *i.e.* QUADRAGÍNTA] MANÉNTIUM
USQUE AD TERMINOS QUAE AD EUM PERTINENT
CUM OMNIBUS AD SE PERTINENTIBUS
CUM CAMPIS SILUIS PRÁTIS ET MARISCO
UT TAM TU QUAM POSTERI TUI TENEATIS POSSIDEATIS
IIII **E**T QUAECUMQUE UOLUERIS DE EÁDEM FACERE TERRA
LIBERAM HABEÁTIS POTESTATEM
V **A**CTUM MENSE MARTIO
VI ET TESTES CONPETENTI NUMERO UT SUBSCRÍBERENT ROGAUI
VII **S**I QUIS CONTRA HANC DONATIONIS KARTULAM UENIRE TEMPTAUERIT AUT CORRUMPERE

33 Sawyer, no. 1171. Chaplais, 'Diplomas', pp. 78–83 and pl. iv. Birch, no. 81. *Ancient Charters*, pl. 2. Lowe, *English Uncial*, pl. xxii. *Chartae Latinae Antiquiores*, no. 187 pp. 32–3. Webster and Backhouse, *The Making of England*, no. 28.

ANTE OMNIPOTENTEM DEUM ET IHESUM XPISTUM FILIUM
EIUS ET SPĪRĬTŪM SĀNCTŬM
ID EST INSEPARĀBĬLĒM TRĪNĬTĀTĒM
SCIAT SÉ CONDEMNÁTUM ET SEPARATUM AB OMNI
SOCIETÁTE XPĪSTĬĀNĀ
MANENTEM HANC KARTULAM DONATIONIS IN SUA
NIHILŌMĬNŪS FĪRMĬTĀTĒ .

VIII ET UT FIRMUM[b] ET INCŌNCŬSSŪM SĪT DŌNŬM
TERMINI SUNT AUTEM ISTI HUIUS TERRAE[c] CUM QUÍBUS
ACCÍNGITUR

VIIII AB ORIENTE ÞRĪTŎLĂ BŬRNĂ

X AB AQUILONE CĘNTINCES TRÍOÞ ĒT HĀNCHĒM STĔDĔ

XI AB AUSTRALE FLÚMĒN TĀMĪSĀ

XII **S**I QUIS AUTEM HANC DONATIONEM AUGĔRĔ UŎLŬĔRĪT
AUGEAT DEUS BONA SUA IN REGIŌNĔ UĪUŌRŬM
CUM SANCTIS SÚIS SINE FĪNĔ ĀMĒN :,

I + **E**GO SEBBI REX EASTSAXANORUM[d] PRO CONFIRMATIONE SUBSCRIPSI .
II **E**GO OEDELRAEDUS DONATOR SUBSCRIPSI .
III + **E**GO ERCNUUALDUS EPISCOPUS CONSENSI ET SUBSCRIPSI .
IIII **E**GO UUILFRIDUS EPISCOPUS CONSENSI ET SUBSCRIPSI .
V + **E**GO HAEDDE EPISCOPUS CONSENSI ET SUBSCRIPSI .
VI **E**GO GUDA PRESBITER ET ABBAS CONSENTIENS SUBSCRIPSI
VII +**E**GO EGCBALDUS PRESBITER ET ABBAS CONSENSI ET SUBSCRIPSI
VIII + **E**GO HAGONA PRESBITER ET ABBAS CONSENTIENS SUBSCRIPSI
VIIII + **E**GO HOOC PRESBITER ET ABBAS CONSENTIENS SUBSCRIPSI

X SIG+NUM MANUS SEBBI REGIS
XI SIG+NUM MANUS SIGIHEARDI REGIS
XII SIG+NUM MANUS SUEBREDI REGIS

De terra quam donauit Odil redus .·. xl. manentium +.
Fundacio mon[asterii] de Bark[in]ge
Þis is seo boc to Bercingon .

a HEDILBURGE. b FIRMA. c TAERRE. d EASTSAX̄.

I +In the name of Our Lord Jesus Christ, the Saviour,
as many times as we are seen to offer something to Your holy and venerable places
we give back Your own things to You, we do not grant our own things.

II On which account I, Æthelræd, parent of Sebbi in the province of the East Saxons,
by [my] own will, in healthy mind, and by sound counsel,
to you, Æthelburh, abbess,
for the increase of your monastery, which is called 'Bedda's Ham',
I hand over perpetually.

III And I transfer from my right to yours the land
which is named 'Ricings' Ham', 'Buda's Ham', 'Decca's Ham', 'Angenlabe's Ham',
and in the field in the wood which is called 'Widmund's Field'
seventy-five [altered to 'forty'] hides which are joined together,
the things which pertain to it [sc. the field] as far as the bounds,
with all things pertaining to it,
with fields, woods, meadows, and marsh,
so that you as well as your successors may hold, may possess.
IIII And whatever things you may wish to do concerning the same land
you may have free power.
V Executed in the month of March.
VI And I have asked witnesses in a fitting number that they may subscribe [lit. 'write below'].
VII If any one should attempt to come against or corrupt this little charter of donation,
before the omnipotent God and Jesus Christ His Son and the Holy Spirit,
that is, the inseparable Trinity,
let him know himself condemned and separated from all Christian society,
this little charter of donation remaining nonetheless in its own effect [or 'validity'].
VIII And that the gift may be firm and unshaken
these, however, are the bounds of this land, with which it is girded round.
VIIII From the east 'Writola Bourn'.
X From the north 'Centinc's Tree' and 'Hanchem Stead'.
XI From the south the River 'Thames'.
XII If any one, however, should wish to increase this donation,
may God increase his own goods in the country of living men
with His own saints without end. Amen.

I +I, Sebbi, King of East Saxons, have subscribed for confirmation.
II I, Æthelræd the giver, have subscribed.
III +I, Eorconweald, bishop, have consented and subscribed.
IIII I, Wilfrid, bishop, have consented and subscribed.
V +I, Haedde, bishop, have consented and subscribed.
VI I, Guda, priest and abbot, consenting have subscribed.
VII +I, Ecgbald, priest and abbot, have consented and subscribed.
VIII +I, Hagona, priest and abbot, consenting have subscribed.
VIIII +I, Hooc, priest and abbot, consenting have subscribed.

X Si+gn of the hand of Sebbi the King.
XI Si+gn of the hand of Sigeheard the King.
XII Si+gn of the hand of Swæfræd the King.

Concerning the land which Odilred gave ∴ 40 hides +.
Foundation of the monastery of Barking
This is the charter for Barking.

Words and ideas have been arranged in chiastic and parallel patterns:

A1	Domini
A2	sanctis
A3	uestris
A4	ego Hodilredus parens Sebbi prouincia Eastsexanorum
A5	consensu
B	uoluntate
C	augmentum
D	trado et de meo iure in tuo transscribo
E1	terram
E2	Ricinga Haam, Budin Haam, Dęccan Haam, Angenlabes Haam, Uuidmundes Felt
F	terminos
G	donationis
H	kartulam
I	corrumpere
J	omnipotentem Deum, Ihesum Xpistum Filium, Spiritum Sanctum
J'	id est inseparabilem Trinitatem
I'	manentem
H'	kartulam
G'	donationis
F'	termini
E'1	terrae
E'2	Ƿritola Burna, Cęntinces Trioƿ, Hanchem Stede, Tamisa
D'	hanc donationem
C'	augere
B'	uoluerit
A'1	Deus
A'2	sanctis
A'3	suis
A'4	ego Sebbi rex Eastsax̄ … ego Oedelraedus
A'5	consensi.

This charter was composed in the tradition we have observed above, as suggested by the twelve sentences and twelve witnesses and thirty-three lines and 222 words, of which the central stand at the centre of the central seventeenth line. The spelling is nearly faultless, with only three trivial errors. The grammar and syntax are faultless. As in other charters of thirty-three lines, thirty exhibit clausular rhythms. One, line 2, ends in a hexameter verse rhythm, and two, lines 12 and 27, end in the rhythm of the *cursus tardus*. The charter was designed to protect the donation from what happened to it. At some point the nuns of Barking must have been forced to alienate thirty-five hides, retaining only forty of the original seventy-five. Someone altered the appearance of the charter of donation, erasing .LXXU. and writing .XL., without understanding the infixed authenticating devices. From the beginning of the charter proper, from | *quotiens* to LXXU, that is, *septuaginta quinque* | inclusive, there are exactly seventy-five words.

The handwriting changes between lines 26 and 27, as does the spelling, the first scribe writing *Hodilredus* and *Eastsexanorum* and the second *Oedelraedus* and *Eastsāx*, the first scribe using *uu* in *Uuidmundes* and the second using Old English *wynn* in *Ƿritola* and *Triop*. Two attestations by Sebbi may suggest that the end of this charter is not exactly like the original. But the chiastic disposition of words implies that the two scribes, obviously early, were copying an even earlier authentic document.

In that earlier document the dative case of the recipient's name was presumably spelled correctly *HEDILBURGAE*, which bears a numerical value of 8+5+4+9+10+2+19+16+7+1+15 or 86. From | *quotiens* to | *tibi Hedilburgae* there are eighty-six syllables.

Sawyer dates this charter to the period '685 x 694, probably 690 x 693'. Keynes dates it to the period 676 x 696. After noting the features it shares with the authentic charters considered above, composition in thirty-three lines with thirty clausular, one hexameter, and two cursus rhythms, and a composition of twelve sentences confirmed by twelve witnesses, one might infer from the numbers of syllables and crosses, 1+529+148+9, a date of 687.

XI. SWÆFRÆD KING OF THE EAST SAXONS TO WEALDHERE BISHOP OF LONDON WITH CONFIRMATION BY TWO MERCIAN KINGS

Here follows a charter, extant in London, British Library, MS Cotton Augustus II.82, dated 13 June 704, from Swæfræd King of the East Saxons to Wealdhere Bishop of London.[34]

I +**In** nomine Domini nostri Ihesu Xpisti Saluatóris
II **Q**uamuis solus sermo sufficeret ad téstimónium
Attamen pro cautella futurórum témporum
ne quis forte posterum fraudulentum[a] ignorantiae piaculum pérperam incúrrat .
Idcirco scedulis saltim uilibus pro ampliore firmitátis suppleménto[b]
necessarium réor adnéctere .
III **Q**uapropter **E**go Sueabræd rex Eástsaxonórum
Et **E**go Pæogthath cum licentia Ædelrédi regis cómes[c]
aliquantulum agri partem pro remedio **a**nimárum nostrárum
Uualdhario **E**piscopo **i**n dominio **d**onáre **d**ecréuimus
id est .XXX. cassatorum **in** loco **q**ui dícitur Tuícan Hom
In prouincia quae[d] nuncupátur Middelseáxan

34 Sawyer, no. 65. Birch, no. 111. *Ancient Charters*, pl. 3. *Chartae Latinae Antiquiores*, no. 188 pp. 36–7.

IIII **H**aec[e] autem terra his locorum limítibus **d**esignátur
V **A**b oriente et austro flumine Támisæ términáta
VI **A** septemtrione plaga torrente cuius uocabulum est Fisces Burna **.**
VII **P**ossessionem autem huius terrae[f] taliter ut súpra díximus
Cum campis sationalibus pascuálibus prátis
palludibus piscariis[g] fluminibus **C**lusúris
omnibus quibus[d] ad eam pértinéntibus
in dominio supra dicti **e**píscopi pòssidéndam[h] **.**
perpetuale iúre tradídimus
VIII **E**t liberam habeat potestatem agendi **q**uodcúmque uoluerit **.**
VIIII Porro ut firmior huius donationis largitio iúgiter sèruarétur
etiam téstes adiúnximus
Quorum nomina subter tenéntur insérta **.**
X **S**i **q**uis uero successórum nostrórum
hanc donationis nostrae[i] munificentiam **au**gere et amplificáre maluerit **.**
Augeat Dominus partem eíus **i**n líbro uítae[j] **.**
XI **S**i quis e **d**iuerso quod absit **.** tyrannica potestate fretus infríngere temptáuerit **.**
sciat se ante tribunal Xpisti tremibundum ratiónem redditúrum
XII **M**aneatque nihilominus[k] **i**n sua firmitáte haec[e] kártulá[l]
scripta **A**nno **a**b incarnatione Domini nostri DCC.IIII. indictióne.II. [i.e. secúnda]
tertia decima die mensis Iunii quod est ídus Iúnii //

I + **E**go Coenredus rex Mercensium hanc terram Ƿaldhario **E**piscopo pro remedio animae meae[m]
in **d**ominio **d**onare **d**ecreui **i**n loco **q**ui dicitur Tuiccan Ham
Et libenti animo propria manu **C**rucem infixi
II + **E**go Headda **E**piscopus consensi et subscripsi
III + **E**go Cotta abbas consensi et subscripsi
IIII + **E**go Suebrædus rex Eastsaxonum propria manus
V + **E**go Peohthat signum manus inposui
VI + **E**go Friodored signum manus
VII + Coenheard signum manus
VIII + Cudræd signum manus
VIIII + Uilloc signum manus
X + Eadred signum
XI + Cymmi signum
XII + Pagara signum

+ **E**go Ciolred [rex] Mercensium hanc **d**onationem **q**uam ante **d**onauit propinqus meus Coenrædus rex
et ego confirmaui in loco Arcencale et signum sanctae crucis expressi
+ Ælric signum manus
+ Lulla signum manus
+ Cynric signum manus
+ Eadberht signum
+ Sceftƿine signum

+ Ƿulfhat signum
+ Tuduna signum
Tuicanham
Suebred Rex dedit Tuickenham Waldhario episcopo. Latine.

a fraudulentam. b supplimento. c comis. d quæ. e hæc. f terræ. g piscu⌐a¬riis. h possidendum. i nostræ. j uitæ. k nil ho / minus. l kartala. m anime meæ.

I + In the name of Our Lord Jesus Christ, the Saviour.
II Although speech alone may suffice for testimony,
yet for protection of future times,
lest anyone by chance should by mistake incur a subsequent fraudulent sin of ignorance,
for that reason in schedules [*i.e.* sheets of parchment], even vile ones, for the greater fulfilment of validity
I am considering fixing something necessary.
III On which account I, Swæfræd, King of the East Saxons,
and I, Pæogthath the Eorl, with the licence of Æthelræd the King,
have decided to give a certain little part of a field for the cure of our souls
to Wealdhere the Bishop in right of lordship,
that is, thirty hides, in the place which is called 'Twicca's Ham' [or 'Ham at the river-fork']
in the province which is named 'Middle Saxons'.
IIII This land, moreover, is marked out by these limits of places.
V Bounded from the east and south by the river 'Thames'.
VI From the northern region by the torrent whose name is 'Bourn of the Fish'.
VII Possession, however, of this land, such as we have said above,
with arable fields, pastures, meadows, swamps,
fish ponds, rivers, enclosures,
all these things pertaining to it
to be possessed in right of lordship of the above said bishop,
we hand over in perpetual right.
VIII And he should have free power of doing whatever he may wish.
VIIII Furthermore, that bestowal of this donation be kept firmer continually,
we have adjoined witnesses
whose names are held inserted below.
X But if anyone of our successors
should prefer to increase and amplify this munificence of our donation,
may the Lord increase his part in the book of life.
XI If, on the other hand, which God forbid, anyone strengthened by tyrannical power should attempt to infringe [it],
let him know himself bound to give back an account before the fearsome tribunal of Christ.
XII Let this little charter remain nonetheless in its own effect [or 'validity'],
written in the year from the Incarnation of Our Lord 704 in the second indiction
on the thirteenth day of the month of June, which is the ides of June.

I + I, Coenræd, King of the March men, have decided to give in the right of lordship to Wealdhere the Bishop for the cure of my soul this land in the place which is called 'Twicca's Ham', and with a willing mind with my own hand I have infixed a cross.
II + I, Headde the Bishop, have consented and subscribed.
III + I, Cotta the Abbot, have consented and subscribed.
IIII + I, Swæfræd, King of the East Saxons, my own hand.
V + I, Peohthat, have imposed the sign of the hand.
VI + I, Frithuræd, the sign of the hand.
VII + Coenheard, the sign of the hand.
VIII + Cuðræd, the sign of the hand.
VIIII + Uilloc, the sign of the hand.
X + Eadræd, the sign.
XI + Cymmi, the sign.
XII + Pagara, the sign.

+ I, Ceolræd, [King] of the March men, have also confirmed in the place 'Arcencale' this donation which my relative Coenræd the King gave before, and I have impressed the sign of the holy cross.
+ Ælric, the sign of the hand.
+ Lulla, the sign of the hand.
+ Cynric, the sign of the hand.
+ Eadbeorht, the sign.
+ Sceaftwine, the sign.
+ Wulfhad, the sign.
+ Tuduna, the sign.

Twica's Ham.
Swæfræd the King gave 'Twickenham' to Wealdhere the Bishop. In Latin.

This charter contains twelve sentences, thirty-three lines of text, 222 words, and confirmation by twelve original witnesses, whose number was later increased to a score. Of thirty-three lines thirty end in clausular rhythms. One, line 32, ends in a hexameter verse rhythm, and two, lines 6 and 29, end in the cursus rhythms *tardus* and *dispondeus dactylicus*.

AN ALFREDIAN CHARTER

XII. ALFRED KING OF THE ANGLES AND SAXONS TO WERFERTH BISHOP OF WORCESTER

Here follows the text of a charter, extant in London, British Library, MS Cotton Tiberius A.XIII, folios 18–19, that conveys land in London from King Alfred to Bishop Werferth in A.D. 889.[35]

35 Sawyer, no. 346. Birch, no. 561.

LUNDEN

I + Sedulo namque nonnullis et maxime per instantis uite turbidam discordie rabiem .
in hac decrepita finis mundialis canitie contíngere sóle*t*
quod simplicem memorialis precordii oculum turbines obliuiose obscenitatis quatiéntes reuérber*ant* :
seu nebule neglegentiarum nubiferis depriuationum fuscationibus : a recte possessionis iure radiantem . iustitie Phébum obnúbil*ant* :

II Quapropter necesse cuilibet homini est ut literatoriis apicibus omnia adquisita . seu possessa . ob presentium siue succedentium cautelam . que a catholicis uel heroicis uiris cuiuslibet persone maioris minorisue . potestatis Deo eiusque sanctis per celorum celsitudinem tradita su*nt*
Etiam testimonio et roboratione ipsorum firme rationis série firmé*ntur* . 5
rectoque caraxantis stilo in scédulis noté*ntur* ;

III Anno igitur postquam almifica celestini luminis gemma per agrum uirginalis pudicitie humano generi desiderabilis Mistici Spiraminis specimine enituit octingentesimo . octuagesimo nono . indictione septima cuius denique splendoris et gratie nobis iubáre radiá*nte* 7
Ego Ælfred rex Anglórum et Sáxon*um*
et Æðelred subregulus et patrícius Mèrció*rum*
cum testimonio et licentia seu consensu senatorum episcoporum seu ducum útriusque gén*tis* 10
pro releuatione facinorum nostrorum et pro adquirenda deifice remuneratiónis réquie
Uuer*f*erðo eximio Huicciorum antistiti ad ecclesiam Ueoᵹernensem in Lundónia ùnam cúrte*m*
que uerbotenus ad antiquum petrosum édificiu*m*
id est æt Hƿætmundes Stane a cíuibus àppellátur
a strata publica usque ad murum eiúsdem ciuitá*tis* . 15
Cuius longitudo est perticarum .XXVI.
et latitudo in superiori parte perticarum .XIII. et pedum .VII.
et in inferiori loco perticarum .XI. et pedum .VI.
ad plenam libertatem infra totius rei sempiternáliter pòssidéndum .
in ecclesiasticum iús conscríbi*mus* . 20
et concedéntes doná*mus* .

IIII Et intro urnam et trutinam ad mensurandum in emendo síue uendéndo
ad usum . siue ad necessitatem propriam . et liberam omnímodis hábeat .
et totius debiti . uel pene fiscalis . uel públice réi .
nisi ad dominium episcopi . ecclesie Ueoᵹernensis que intus contingat absolúta persísta*t* . 25

V Si autem foris uel in strata publica seu in ripa emtorali quislibet suórum mercáu*erit* .
iuxta quod rectum sit . thelon ad manum régis súbe*at*
quod si intus in curte predicto quislibet emerit . uél uendíd*erit*
thelon debitum ad manum episcopi supra memoráti reddá*tur* .
et semper quamdiu unde sacri baptismatis populi Anglorum siue Saxonum per fidem Xpistiane religiónis aspergén*tur* . 30
seu ipsorum auctoritatis dominio urbs Lundonia habilis subiaceat ad Ueogernensem ciuitatem súbdita persísta*t* .

VI Contestamur et obsecramus uniuscuiusque personas hominum presentium siue subsequentium . ut hoc nostrum donum inuiolatum et integrum sicut presens pagina testátur permáne*at* .

VII Si qui uero ut non optamus serpentino suggestionis demonice toxico inflati huius tramitis seriem in aliquo *fedáre* temptá*uerint*

nouerint se cum Anna . et Zaphira erebica eterne anathematis machera perforandos nisi . prius digna satisfactione emen*dáre* mal*úerint* .

VIII Hec autem sunt nomina illorum qui huic nostre donationi testes et consentiéntes *fuérunt* .

et trophico sancte crucis uexillo roborantes propriis mánibus sùbscrips*érunt* ;

I +Ego Ælfred rex Anglorum et Saxonum hanc donationem confirmans signo crucis subscribo .

II +Ego Æþelred subregulus et patricius Merciorum hanc donationem signo crucis subscripsi [.]

III +Ego Æþelflæd . consensi .

IIII +Ego Uulfred . episcopus consensi .

V +Ego Alhard . episcopus consensi .

VI +Ego Uuærfrid episcopus . consensi .

VII +Ego Deneuulf . episcopus . consensi .

VIII +Ego Uulfsige episcopus consensi .

1 uitę discordię canitię. 3 nebulę depriua . / tionum iustitię phoebum. 4 atquisita quę. 7 cęlestini pudicitię .VII. gratię. 11 reuelatione requię. 12 uuærfriðo. ęcclesiam. 13 ad ad ædificium. 18 .VI. pedum. 25 quę. 30 saxanum asspargentur. 33 demonicę temptauerint foedare. 34 herebica aeterne. 35 Haec.

LONDON

I +For sincerely for not a few reasons and especially because of the disturbed madness of the discord of the present life, in this decrepit white-haired old age of the end of the world it customarily happens

that the shaking disturbances of oblivious indecency beat back the simple eye of the breast of memory

or clouds of forgetfulnesses with cloud-bearing darkenings of deprivations from the law of correct possession cloud over the radiating sun of justice.

II On which account it is necessary for each man that with literary tips[36] as a cautioning of present or succeeding men all things acquired or possessed, which from catholic or heroic men of whatever personal status, greater or lesser, have been handed over through the height of the heavens to the God of power and His saints

should be confirmed even by witness and corroboration in a succession of these very men of firm reason,

and they should be noted in schedules in a correct style of writing.

III In the year, therefore, the eight-hundredth, eightieth, ninth, in the seventh indiction, after the bountiful gem of celestial light through the field of virginal chastity desirable to the human race shone by the embodiment of the Mystic Spirit, the brightness of Whose splendour and grace radiating at last for us,

36 i.e. 'of letters'; by synecdoche 'entire letters'.

I, Alfred King of the Angles and Saxons,
and Æthelræd Underking and Patrician of the Mercians,
with the witness and licence or consent of the senators, bishops, or ealdormen of either race,
for the relieving of our sins and for the rest of godly remuneration to be acquired,
to Werferth the outstanding Bishop of the Hwicce at the church of Worcester one enclosure in London,
which by name At the Ancient Stone Building,
that is, 'At Hwætmund's Stone', is called by the citizens,
from the public street as far as the wall of the same city.
the length of which is twenty-six perches,
and the breadth in the upper part thirteen perches and seven feet,
and in the lower place eleven perches and six feet,
to be possessed eternally to the full liberty of the entire estate within,
we ascribe to ecclesiastical right
and conceding we give.

IIII And within, the urn[37] and the scale for measuring in buying or selling,
for use or for need he should have proper and free in all respects,
and of all debt, either of fiscal penalty or of public business,
except for the domain of the bishop of the church of Worcester, what belongs
within should persist absolved.

V If, however, any of his own men should engage in business in markets or in the public street or on the commercial riverbank,
according to what may be correct the tax should go to the hand of the king;
if within, in the foresaid enclosure, anyone should buy or sell anything,
the tax owed should be given back to the hand of the bishop called to mind above,
and always as long as the waves of sacred baptism through the faith of the Christian religion of the people of the Angles or the Saxons will be sprinkled
or the city of London should lie fit for the dominion of the authority of the same [Angles or Saxons, the property] should persist subject to the city of Worcester.

VI We call to witness and beseech the persons of each of the men present and following after that this our gift should remain inviolate and intact just as the present page bears witness.

VII If, as in truth we do not wish, any men inflated with the serpentine poison of demonic suggestion should attempt to befoul the line of this path [of writing] in any respect,
they should know themselves bound to be pierced through with the single-edged hellish sword of an eternal anathema with Annas and Sapphira, unless they should earlier prefer to make amends with worthy satisfaction.

VIII These, however, are the names of those men who were witnesses and consenters to this our donation
and corroborating with the trophic sign of the holy cross they have written below with their own hands.

I + I Alfred King of the Angles and Saxons confirming this donation with the sign of the cross underwrite.

37 a liquid measure of about three gallons.

II + I Æthelræd Underking and Patrician of the Mercians have underwritten this donation with the sign of the cross.
III + I Æthelflæd have consented.
IIII + I Wulfræd Bishop have consented.
V + I Ealheard Bishop have consented.
VI + I Werferth Bishop have consented.
VII + I Denewulf Bishop have consented.
VIII + I Wulfsige Bishop have consented.

The script of the charter is Caroline minuscule but for English names in Insular minuscule script, particularly the letters *æ*, *f*, *ᵹ*, long *r*, long *s*, *ð*, and *ƿ* in *Ælfred* 8, *Æðelred* 9, *Uuærfriðo* 12, *Uueoᵹernensem* 12 and 31, *æt Hƿætmundes Stane* 14, and *Uueoᵹernensis* 25.

The spelling of this copy of the charter is good, but probably changed slightly from that of the original. As *ę caudata in canitię* 1 is inappropriate, and as alliteration of *celorum celsitudinem* 4 implies *e* rather than *ae* in *celorum* one infers that the original exhibited throughout *e* for Classical *ae* and *oe*. This marks the composition as orthographically different, as it is stylistically different, from the compositions of known Latin authors at the Alfredian court, particularly John the Old Saxon and Asser of Saint David's.[38]

The drafter of this charter arranged his words and ideas by chiasmus and parallelism.

4 A1 cuilibet
4 A2 homini
4 A3 presentium siue succedentium
5 B testimonio
8 C1 Anglorum et Saxonum
12 C2 ad ecclesiam Uueogernensem in Lundonia
12 D1 unam curtem
22 D2 in emendo siue uendendo
24 D3 debiti
25 D4 ad dominium episcopi ecclesie Uueogernensis
26 E Si autem foris
28 E' quod si intus
28 D'1 in curte predicto
28 D'2 emerit uel uendiderit
29 D'3 debitum
29 D'4 ad manum episcopi supra memorati
30 C'1 Anglorum et Saxonum
31 C'2 urbs Lundonia habilis subiaceat ad Uueogernensem ciuitatem
32 B' contestamur
32 A'1 uniuscuiusque
32 A'2 hominum
32 A'3 presentium siue subsequentium

38 *British Books in Biblical Style*, pp. 365–445, 493–7; *Cambro-Latin Compositions*, pp. 84–94. The Latinity of this charter resembles that of texts composed during the reign of Alfred's grandson Æthelstan more nearly than it resembles any other text from the Alfredian court.

The proem is arranged *per cola et commata* in seven rhyming lines that exhibit the ratio 4:3 once, aaaa bbc, and the ratio 2:1 twice, 4:2:1, aaaa bb c: *-t -ant -ant -nt, -entur -entur, -ante*. The date of the charter in the seventh indiction is consistent with the seven lines of the proem. The year of the grant, A.D. 889, is consistent with the 889 characters from + *Sedulo* to *radiante* inclusive.

Among the earliest extant genuine English charters, composed between A.D. 679 and 704, several early Kentish and Mercian compositions exhibit twenty-two or thirty-three lines of text and 222 words. This charter contains eight sentences, and it is attested by eight witnesses. It contains forty-four lines of text and 444 words and crosses from + *Sedulo* to *subscripsi* inclusive.[39] The number 444 divides by extreme and mean ratio at 274 and 170, at the beginning of the description of the property conveyed, *unam* | *curtem* 12, and at the crux of the chiasmus at part E *Si* | *autem foris* 26.

In the description of the property conveyed there are twenty-six words from *que uerbotenus* 13 to *perticarum* | *XXVI* 16. In line 17 *XIII* is the thirteenth word from the end of the bounds. Also in line 17 there are seven words before | *et pedum VII*. In line 18 there are six words before | *et pedum VI*.

CONCLUSIONS

The Gregorian missionaries brought with them at the end of the sixth century a culture of literacy. They imported to Anglo-Saxon England *codices plurimos*, some of which were known to the Venerable Bede in the eighth century.[40] The Canterbury historian Thomas Elmham published a list of books which were believed in the fifteenth century to have survived from the time of Saint Augustine.[41] Some survive to this day.[42] Æthelbeorht, the first Christian King of the men of Kent, produced, probably with the help of the Gregorian missionaries, a code of laws in Old English, which Bede described as composed *iuxta exempla Romanorum*, and which survives in a twelfth-century copy in the *Textus Roffensis*.[43] It is not unreasonable to infer that Augustine and his colleagues introduced into such a milieu the idea of recording conveyances of

39 For other examples of play on the number 444 see Howlett, *English Origins*, pp. 132–5, *Cambro-Latin Compositions*, pp. 153–5, and *Caledonian Craftsmanship* chapter V.I.

40 Bede, *Historia Ecclesiastica* I XXIX.

41 *Historia Monasterii Monasterii S. Augustini Cantuariensis by Thomas of Elmham*, ed. C. Hardwick, Rolls Series VIII (London: Longman, Brown, Green, Longmans, and Roberts, 1858), pp. 96–9.

42 Lowe, *English Uncial*, p. 7.

43 Bede, *Historia Ecclesiastica* II V. F. Liebermann ed., *Die Gesetze der Angelsachsen* (Halle: Max Niemeyer, 1903), vol. I pp. 3–8, transl. *English Historical Documents*, vol. I pp. 357–8. *Textus Roffensis*, ed. P. Sawyer, Early English Manuscripts in Facsimile VII (Copenhagen: Rosenkilde and Bagger, 1957), vol. I fols 1–3v. Webster and Backhouse, *The Making of England*, no. 25. For analysis see *British Books in Biblical Style*, pp. 257–62.

land in written charters. But, if such charters ever existed, none has survived. The oldest extant English charters issue from the time of Archbishop Theodore, and even the earliest show that they belong to an Insular tradition.

The eleven early charters we have considered claim to have issued from five Kentish kings, Hlothhere, Eadric, Swæfheard, Oswine, and Wihtræd; two East Saxon kings, Sebbi and Swæfræd, and one East Saxon layman, Hodilred or Æthelræd; and two Mercian kings, Coenræd and Ceolræd. They proclaim their beneficiaries as Abbot Beorhtweald of Reculver, Abbot Hadrian of Saint Peter's in Canterbury, Abbess Eabbe of Minster-in-Thanet, the church of Saint Mary at Lyminge, Abbess Hedilburg or Æthelburh of Barking, and Bishop Wealdhere of London. King Wihtræd instructs Abbess Eabbe explicitly to keep the charter he has 'dictated'. The sites belong to different ecclesiastical jurisdictions, Canterbury and London. The dates span a period of twenty-five years from 679 to 704. Topographical names like Thanet and Sturry and Thames are recorded sometimes in English, sometimes in Latin. Some charters are written in English uncial script, some in half-uncial, and others in Insular minuscule, but even those in a single script exhibit different hands and different spellings of vernacular names.

Of the twelve charters considered in this chapter ten exhibit fixed numbers of sentences, usually bearing a relation to a number of elements in the witness list, twelve in the first, second, seventh, tenth, and eleventh, eight in the twelfth, six in the fourth, fifth, and eighth, three in the sixth. Of the eleven early charters considered here seven, the first, second, third, fifth, seventh, tenth, and eleventh, contain thirty-three lines of text. Two, the fourth and the eighth, contain half of that number, sixteen and one-half. One, the sixth, contains two-thirds of that number, twenty-two. Four of them, the first, second, fifth, and seventh, contain 240 words, and two, the fourth and eighth, contain half of that number, 120. The two non-Kentish charters, the tenth and eleventh, contain 222 words each.[44] One, the sixth, contains a Biblically significant number, 144.[45] Of those containing thirty-three lines four, the first, second, fourth, and eleventh, exhibit thirty lines with clausular rhythms and three lines without clausular rhythms, usually one hexameter verse ending and two cursus rhythms, a feature shared with the prose of the Romano-Britons Patrick (*ob.* 461) and Faustus of Riez (*ob.* c490), the Irishman Aileranus Sapiens (*ob.* 665), and the Englishman Wilfrid.[46]

44 For other examples of play on the numbers 22, 222, and 2222 see Howlett, *Book of Letters*, p. 43, 'Five Experiments', pp. 7–8, 15–18, 27–9, 46, *Cambro-Latin Compositions*, pp. 126, 133, 'Insular Acrostics', p. 43, '*Vita I Sanctae Brigitae*', pp. 1–23.

45 For other examples of play on the number 144 see below pp. 66, 91, and Howlett, *Book of Letters*, pp. 43, 46, 'Five Experiments', pp. 17, 47, 'Seven Studies', p. 53, *Celtic Latin Tradition*, pp. 21, 25, 71, 264, *British Books in Biblical Style*, pp. 19, 26, *Cambro-Latin Compositions*, pp. 133–4, 137.

46 Howlett, *Cambro-Latin Compositions*, pp. 4–15; 'Seven Studies', pp. 6–11; 'Insular Latin Writers' Rhythms', pp. 88–92. Leofranc Holford-Strevens suggests that thirty may represent the years Christ lived under the Law and three the years of the new

Regardless of whether one should imagine these charters as compositions by royal notaries or by ecclesiastical notaries or by the beneficiaries, there is so much variety in them that no one can suppose they were all drafted by one man or in one place. The likely inference is that more than one or two literate seventh-century Englishmen understood the conventions, which entailed both adherence to rules scrupulously observed and generation of form anew each time, without copying a formulary. We may infer as a rule of thumb that copying is characteristic not of composers in this tradition, but of later tinkerers and forgers.

These charters bear no seals, no autograph signatures, no autograph signs manual. They depend for their acceptance as genuine documents upon understanding of their multiple infixed devices, an understanding widespread but not universal. If these devices were not recognizable by many they would have no power to authenticate genuine compositions. If they were recognizable by everyone they would have no power to deter or reveal fraudulent compositions. As no extant charter is arranged *per cola et commata*, no nine-word clause marked as ninth from the beginning and ninth from the end, nor are the rhythms marked, nor clausulae visibly distinguished from cursus rhythms and hexameter endings, nor are chiastic and parallel passages flagged, these devices had to be recognized by abstraction, without any of the visual aids or scansion marks or numbered lines employed in this analysis.[47]

If we compare these charters with contemporary Latin monuments, inscriptions from Rome and notarial instruments from Ravenna and charters from Merovingian Gaul, the English charters emerge from comparison favourably, as orthographically and grammatically and syntactically correct, elegant in their rhythmic prose, punctilious in small detail, consistent in comprehensive design, written in legible, competent, even beautiful scripts. The present writer knows of no model from Rome or Ravenna or anywhere else in Ostrogothic Italy, nor from Merovingian Gaul, nor from Visigothic Spain, that would account for the combined features of these English charters. How, then, is one to explain such remarkable documents composed to so high a standard?

Part of an answer is that from the beginnings of British literary history the standards of composition in Latin were high. For analysis of works by the fifth-century Romano-Britons Pelagius, Patrick, and Faustus of Riez, at various points of the literary register, see *The Celtic Latin Tradition of Biblical Style*, *The Book of Letters of Saint Patrick the Bishop*, and *Cambro-Latin Compositions: Their*

dispensation of His ministry. The point of such a device must be to imply mastery of three different forms of rhythm in the proportion 3(0):2:1.

47 For recognition by abstraction of these features in longer and more complex texts of the eleventh and twelfth centuries see Howlett, 'Arithmetic Rhythms in Latin Letters', *Archivum Latinitatis Medii Aevi* LVI (1998), pp. 193–225, and in texts of the twelfth and fourteenth centuries, 'Sixes and Sevens in Anglo-Latin Prologues', *Mittellateinisches Jahrbuch* (forthcoming).

Competence and Craftsmanship.[48] Exactly 130 years after withdrawal of Roman civilian and military administrators from Britain Gildas Sapiens, in A.D. 540, wrote *De Excidio Britanniae* in difficult finely wrought Latin that compares favourably in lexical and syntactical and stylistic respects with the prose of his Continental successor Gregory of Tours.[49] Sixty years later Columban of Bangor alluded to the elegant correspondence between Gildas and another Briton named Vinniau, celebrated as founder of the monastery of Clonard, whose death is recorded under 12 December in liturgical calendars, under the year 549 in the *Annals of Ulster*.[50] Evidence of continued intellectual acuity and literary accomplishment among Welshmen of the seventh century survives in the *Orationes Moucani*, rhyming rhythmical Latin prayers,[51] and in monumental inscriptions in competent quantitative and syllabic metres.[52]

In the letter of A.D. 600 mentioned above Columban of Bangor, the first Irish author whose Latin works survive under his own name, displays his argumentative skills with wit and panache in a *tour de force* that emerges favourably from comparison with the works of Gregory the Great, to whom he addressed it.[53] A note about Columban's teacher Mo-Sinu maccu Min, Sinlanus Abbot of Bangor (*ob*. 610),[54] a computistical poem of A.D. 645,[55] two works by Laidcenn mac Baíth Bannaig (*ob*. 661),[56] seven works by and for Cummianus Longus (*ob*. 662),[57] three works by Aileranus Sapiens (*ob*. 665),[58] and three works by Virgilius Maro Grammaticus[59] illustrate clearly and powerfully the fluent mastery of orthography, grammar, syntax, and style of Latin composition by large numbers of Irishmen during the seventh century.

Soon after 670 Bishop Theodore of Canterbury and Abbot Hadrian of Saint Peter's, Canterbury, established a brilliant school that had no equal in Anglo-Saxon England. In literary terms their most distinguished alumnus was Aldhelm,

48 Howlett, *Celtic Latin Tradition*, pp. 56–65, *Book of Letters*, *passim*, *Cambro-Latin Compositions*, pp. 4–15.

49 Howlett, *Celtic Latin Tradition*, pp. 72–81, *Cambro-Latin Compositions*, pp. 33–56.

50 Howlett, 'Two Works of Saint Columban', pp. 27–35; *Celtic Latin Tradition*, pp. 82–91; 'Insular Latin Writers' Rhythms', pp. 57–9; *Cambro-Latin Compositions*, pp. 42–3.

51 Howlett, '*Orationes Moucani*: Early Cambro-Latin Prayers', *Cambridge Medieval Celtic Studies* XXIV (1992), pp. 55–74, and *Celtic Latin Tradition*, pp. 193–213, superseded by *Cambro-Latin Compositions*, pp. 57–68.

52 Howlett, 'Insular Latin Writers' Rhythms', pp. 63–4, 77–81; 'Literate Culture of "Dark Age" Britain', *British Archaeology* no. 33 (April 1998), pp. 10–11; *Cambro-Latin Compositions*, pp. 17–32.

53 As above n. 50.

54 Howlett, 'Five Experiments', pp. 1–3, and Insular Latin Writers' Rhythms', pp. 59–60.

55 Howlett, 'Seven Studies', pp. 1–6.

56 Howlett, 'Five Experiments', pp. 6–18.

57 Howlett, 'Seven Studies', pp. 32–50.

58 *Ibid*., pp. 6–20.

59 *Ibid*., pp. 50–7.

the first man among all Germanic peoples to achieve the status of Latin author whose works survive under his own name, who became Abbot of Malmesbury about 675 and first Bishop of Sherborne from 705 until his death in 709. The most articulate tribute to the literary standards and achievements of the Irish is the polemic of Letters to Heahfrith and Wihtfrith, in which Aldhelm attempted to dissuade these young Englishmen from studying in Ireland by extolling the virtues of Theodore and Hadrian and displaying the form of learning inculcated in their school.[60] We may take this controversialist at his word: he sought less to dispraise the Irish than to praise his own tutors at Canterbury. There was no point whatever in deriding distinguished Hiberno-Latin authors whose texts Aldhelm quotes with the respect they deserve. There was, however, polemic value in addressing subjects not discussed by Irish scholars and in surpassing their stylistic ambitions. The early charters we have been examining exhibit functional elegance of diplomatic instruments identical with the literary elegance of learned works from the school of Theodore and Hadrian. They are composed in the same Biblical style, one purpose of which is to fix thought and expression in irreformable documents, their authenticity and integrity protected by multiple infixed error-detection and error-correction devices, and another purpose of which is to exhibit the intellectual acuity and suppleness of the composers.

By the time Englishmen began to practise this form of composition Welshmen and Irishmen had already produced a prodigious literature in it. Observing the same conventions yet producing idiosyncratic works, no two authors in Cambro-Latin or Hiberno-Latin or Anglo-Latin literature are in the least degree confusable. All three traditions went from strength to strength. The number of centres from which we know such works emerged in Wales and Ireland is astonishingly large, that in England smaller, but remarkable. Within half a century of the founding of the Canterbury school Bede had established his reputation as a formidable scholar at Wearmouth-Jarrow. One need not rehearse details of the Continental missions of Willibrord from Rath Melsige, of Uynfreth or Boniface from Wessex, of Alcuin from York, and scores of Irish *peregrini* in the Carolingian schools of the eighth century and later. These men are responsible not only for transmission to the Continent of the form of composition we have been considering, but for imposing on Continental speakers of devolving Latin and evolving Romance vernaculars their Insular standards of correct Latinity.[61] In these early English charters we see clear signs of a linguistic and literary tradition of immense importance, not only for the study of Insular diplomatic practice, but for the intellectual history of Europe.

60 As above p. 20 n. 4.

61 D.R. Howlett, 'A Modest Proposal for Education in Ireland', *Classics Ireland* III (1996), pp. 97–108. For a comparable argument based upon other evidence see Roger Wright, *Late Latin and Early Romance in Spain and Carolingian France* (Liverpool: Francis Cairns, 1982).

III

WELSH CHARTERS

Manuscripts associated with Llandeilo Fawr and Llancarfan and Llandaff preserve texts of Cambro-Latin charters. Of these the third group have been comprehensively revised and edited by the twelfth-century compilers of the *Liber Landauensis*;[1] the second have been inserted into a twelfth-century copy of Lifris of Llancarfan's *Vita Sancti Cadoci*;[2] but the first, which have been inserted into margins of the Gospels now at Saint Chad's Cathedral in Lichfield, are original authorial texts with which we may begin consideration of the Welsh tradition.[3]

The Gospels in Lichfield Cathedral MS 1 are written in Insular half-uncial script of the eighth century and decorated with illuminations in Insular style of the same date. By about A.D. 820 they were on the altar of Saint Teilo, probably at Llandeilo Fawr in Carmarthenshire, where they acquired marginal memoranda in Cambro-Latin and Old Welsh. Some aspects of the high craftsmanship of these compositions have escaped the notice of modern scholars.

1 Michael Lapidge and Richard Sharpe, *A Bibliography of Celtic-Latin Literature 400–1200*, Dictionary of Medieval Latin from Celtic Sources, Ancillary Publications I (Dublin: Royal Irish Academy, 1985) [hereafter *BCLL*], no. 154 p. 50. *The Text of the Book of Llan Dâv Reproduced from the Gwysaney Manuscript*, ed. J. Gwenogvryn Evans and John Rhys (Oxford, 1893, rept National Library of Wales, 1979), pp. 72–8, 121–9, 140–247, 249–75. Wendy Davies, *The Llandaff Charters* (Aberystwyth: National Library of Wales, 1979).

2 *BCLL*, no. 155 p. 50. *Vitae Sanctorum Britanniae et Genealogiae*, ed. and transl. A.W. Wade-Evans, Board of Celtic Studies, University of Wales History and Law Series IX (Cardiff: University of Wales Press, 1944), pp. 124–37.

3 *BCLL*, no. 156 p. 50. Evans and Rhys, *Book of Llan Dâv*, transcripts pp. xliii–xlvii, with facsimiles opposite. The reproductions in the reprint are less clear than those in the edition of 1893. For recent consideration see Douglas Brown, *The Lichfield Gospels*, Pitkin Pictorial Guides and Souvenir Books (London: Pitkin Pictorials, 1982), facsimiles on front cover and pp. 7 and 15, and Dafydd Jenkins and Morfydd E. Owen, 'The Welsh Marginalia in the Lichfield Gospels', *Cambridge Medieval Celtic Studies*, Part I vol. V (1983), pp. 37–66, facsimile pl. A opposite p. 78, Part II vol. VII (1984), pp. 91–120. Paul Russell, *An Introduction to the Celtic Languages*, Longman Linguistics Library (London and New York: Longman, 1995), facsimile on front cover.

I. MEMORANDUM I: GELHI TO SAINT TEILO

At the top of page 141 *Memorandum I* records the presentation of the Gospels to Saint Teilo.

> Ostenditur híc quod emit +gel hi+ filius· ariht iud· hoc· euange
> lium· de cjngal· et dedit· illi pro illo equm· optimum· et dedit
> pro anima sua istum euangelium· deo et sancti teliaui· super altare
> +gel hi+ filius· **A**riht iud··,··, et +cj́ncénn+ filius· grip iud··,

The following arrangement reveals the chiastic structure of words and ideas and the cursus rhythms of the prose.

A1	**O**sténditur hìc quod émit	4	8	21	It is shown here that
A2	+Gelhi+ filius· Árihtiud·	3	8	19+4	Gelli son of Arthudd
B	hoc· euangélium· de Cjngal·	4	9	21+3	bought this Gospel from Cyngal
C	et dedit· ílli pró illo	5	8	18+1	and he gave to him for it
D	équm · óptimum·	2	5	11+2	a very good horse,
C'	et dedit pro ánima súa	5	9	18	and he gave for his own soul
B'	istum euangélium· Déo	3	9	18+1	this Gospel to God
A'1	et Sancti Teliaui· súper altáre	5	12	26+1	even on Saint Teilo's altar.
A'2	+Gelhi+ filius· **Á**rihtiud··,··,	3	8	19+9	Gelli son of Arthudd
	et +Cjncenn+ filius. Grípiud··,	4	8	22+6	and Cyngen son of Gruffudd.
		38	84	193+27	

There is a simple two-part structure of Disposition in lines 1–8 and Attestation in lines 9–10. Compare *hic* in A1 with *super altare* in A'1, *Gelhi filius Arihtiud* in A2 with the same words in A'2, *hoc euangelium* in B with *istum euangelium* in B', *et dedit ... pro* in C with *et dedit pro* in C', disposed round the crux D, *equm optimum*, the price paid for the book.

Every line ends with a good cursus rhythm, *uelox* in line 1, *tardus* in lines 2 and 9, *trispondiacus* in line 3, *planus* in lines 6, 7, 8, 10, and *medius* in lines 4 and 5.

The thirty-eight words about Gelli's presentation of the book divide by extreme and mean ratio at 23 and 15. There are fifteen words between *euangelium* | and | *euangelium*, which divide in turn by the same ratio at 9 and 6, at *pro* | *illo* [*i.e. euangelio*]. There are nine words from the beginning to *euangelium* | and fourteen words from | *euangelium* to the end, together twenty-three words, which divide in turn by the same ratio at 14 and 9. There are seven words from the beginning to *Gelhi filius Arihtiud* | and seven words from | *Gelhi filius Arihtiud* to the end, together fourteen. After the former *Arihtiud* the fourteenth word is | *anima sua*.

The eighty-four syllables about Gelli's presentation of the book divide by extreme and mean ratio at 52 and 32. There are thirty-two syllables from | *euangelium* to | *euangelium*.

Memorandum I conforms with a widespread convention of referring to the principal subject or author or patron at places determined by sesquioctave ratio

9:8 or one-ninth and eight-ninths of a composition. The 38 words divide by 9:8 at 20 and 18, at *equm optimum* | and | *pro anima sua*, by one-ninth and eight-ninths at 4 and 34, at | *Gelhi filius Arihtiud* and *Gelhi filius Arihtiud* |.

In the widely attested earlier form of reckoning letters as numerals the name of the donor *GELHI* bears a numerical value of 7+5+10+8+9 or 39, one more than the number of words in the entire composition.[4] The name of his father *ARIHTIUD* bears a numerical value of 1+16+9+8+18+9+19+4 or 84, exactly the number of syllables in the entire composition. The name *GELHI FILIUS ARIHTIUD* bears a numerical value of 7+5+10+8+9+6+9+10+9+19+17 +1+16+9+8+18+9+19+4 or 193, exactly the number of letters in the entire composition.[5]

The name of the recipient *TELIAU* bears a numerical value of 18+5+10+9 +1+19 or 62. The sentence *et dedit pro anima sua istum euangelium Deo et Sancti Teliaui super altare* contains sixty-two letters.

II. MEMORANDUM II: THE SURREXIT MEMORANDUM

Here follows a transcript of *Memorandum II*. The first part directly follows *Memorandum I* above the main text of the page. The second part appears in the lower margin, where it is preceded and followed by other memoranda.

> **S**urexit tut bulc filius liuit hagener tutri dierchim· tir telih· haioid ilau
> elcu filius gelhig haluidt iuguret amguca^{n}t pel amtanndi ho diued
> dipro tant gener tutrí o guir imguodant irdegion guragun tagc
> rodesit elcu guetig equs tres uache› tres uache nouidligi namin ir
> ni be cás igridu dimedichat guetig bit did braut grefiat gue
> tig nis minn tutbulc hai cenetl in ois oisouð
>
> \+ teliau testis gurgint testis cinhilinn testis spiritus testis› tota familia teliaui› delaicis
> numin map aidan› testis signou map iacou testis berthutis testis **C**inda testis· quicunque custo
> dierit benedictus erit› quicunque frangerit maladictus erit**3**››–'

Let us distinguish Welsh from Latin typographically.[6]

4 For allowance in apparent equality of a margin of one or two see above p. 7 n. 2.

5 For examples of this among the English see above, pp. 21, 25, 32, 35, 41, 47; for other examples among the Welsh, Cornish, Irish, and Scots see below, pp. 66, 73, 77–8, 81, 85–6, 91, 94, 99.

6 The arrangement of the text is mine. The translation is that of Jenkins and Owen, 'Welsh Marginalia', p. 51.

Pars I Dispositio

1 **S**urexit *Tutbulc* filius *Liuit ha* gener Tutri *di erchim ·Tir Telih· hai oid i lau Elcu* filius *Gelhig ha luidt Iuguret.*

2 *Amgucant pel amtanndi ho diued diprotant* gener Tutri *o guir.*

3 *Imguodant ir degion Guragun tagc.*

4 *Rodesit Elcu guetig* equs tres uache, tres uache *nouidligi nam ir ni be cas igridu di medichat guetig bit Did Braut.*

5 *Grefiat guetig nis minn Tutbulc hai cenetl in ois oisou.*

Pars II Attestatio

6 + *Teliau* testis *Gurgint* testis *Cinhilinn* testis Spiritus testis, tota familia Teliaui,

7 De laicis *Numin map Aidan*, testis *Signou map Iacou* testis *Berthutis* testis **C***inda* testis·

Pars III Sanctio

8 Quicunque custodierit benedictus erit,

9 Quicunque frangerit maladictus erit **3**,,–'

Part I Disposition

1 *Tudfwlch* the son *of Llywyd and* the son-in-law of Tudri arose *to claim 'Tir Telych', which was in the hand of Elgu* the son *of Gelli and the tribe of Idwared.*

2 *They disputed long about it; in the end they disjudge* Tudri's son-in-law *by law.*

3 *The goodmen said to each other, 'Let us make peace'.*

4 *Elgu gave afterwards* a horse, three cows, three *newly-calved* cows, *only in order that there might not be hatred between them from the ruling afterwards till the Day of Judgment.*

5 *A document afterwards: Tudfwlch and his kin will not want it for ever and ever.*

Part II Attestation

6 *Teilo* witness, *Gwryn* witness, *Cynhilyn* witness, the Spirit witness, all the household of Teilo.

7 Of the laymen *Nefyn son of Aeddan* witness, *Sywno son of Iago* witness, *Berthudys* witness, *Cynda* witness.

Part III Sanction

8 Whosoever observes it will be blessed.

9 Whosoever breaks it will be cursed.

The memorandum contains nine sentences, five in the Disposition, and four others, two in the Attestation, and two in the Sanction. Divided another way, five of the nine sentences are bilingual in Latin and Welsh, and four are not, two in monoglot Latin, and two in monoglot Welsh. Here is no haphazard or inadvertent slipping from one language into another. The author played with two languages in a memorandum composed by duple ratio 2:1.

Among the five sentences of the Disposition there are two before and two after the central sentence about making peace. Sentences 1 and 4 contain the same number of words, twenty-one. Sentences 2 and 5 contain the same number of words, ten, half as many as sentences 1 and 4. The central sentence contains five words, half as many as sentences 2 and 5.

In sentence 4 the twenty-one words divide into thirds at the latter *tres*. The first seven words divide by sesquitertian ratio 4:3 at the former *tres*, there being three words from *tres* to *tres* inclusive.

In the two sentences of the Attestation the sixth sentence contains eleven words and the seventh sentence fourteen words. Divided another way these two sentences contain eleven words of Welsh and fourteen words of Latin. As there are nine sentences in the entire memorandum, so there are nine witnesses in the Attestation, five clerical and four lay.

The two sentences of the Sanction are syntactically parallel, each containing four words.

The entire memorandum contains exactly one hundred words, of which thirty-four are Latin and sixty-six are Welsh, another duple ratio. There are sixty-seven words in the Disposition and thirty-three in the Attestation and Sanction, another duple ratio.

Jenkins and Owen have inferred reasonably that 'the Elgu who was allowed to use the Gospel book to record proof of his proprietorship of "Tir Telych" was the son of the Gelli who gave the book'.[7] As the thirty-eight words of *Memorandum I* divide by one-ninth and eight-ninths at the name of the man who gave the book, the one hundred words of *Memorandum II* divide by one-ninth at 11, at *Tir Telih* |, the name of the place under consideration.

III. MEMORANDUM III:
RHYS AND LUITH GRETHI TO SAINT TEILO

The text of *Memorandum III* appears in the upper and right margins of page 18.

Ostendit ista scriptjo quod dederunt· ris· et luith grethi· treb gujdauc· imalitiduch
\cimarguith
[i]ejt· hic est census eius· douceint torth· ha maharuin· in irham· ha douceint torth·
\in irgaem· ha huch· ha
[do]uceint mannuclenn· deo et sancto eliudo· deus· testis· saturnnguid· testis· nobís
\testis· guurci· testis· cutulf· testis·· delaicis·
cinguernn· testis·
collbiu· testis· cohor
get· testis· ermin·
testis·· hourod· testis·
quicunque cus
todierit
benedictus
erit· et qui
franxerit
maladictus
erit· a deo··

7 Jenkins and Owen, 'Welsh Marginalia', p. 52.

Let us arrange the text thus.[8]

	Pars I Dispositio			
1	**O**stendit ista scriptjo quod dederunt· *Ris*· et *Luith Grethi*· *Treb Gujdauc*·	11	20	59
2	*i mal i ti duch cimarguithiejt*·	6	9	25
3	hic est census eius·	4	6	16
4	*douceint torth· ha maharuin· in ir ham*·	7	10	30
5	*ha douceint torth· in ir gaem· ha huch*·	8	9	29
6	*ha douceint mannu clenn*·	4	6	20
7	Deo et Sancto Eliudo·	4	9	17
		44	69	196
	Pars II Attestatio			
8	Deus· testis· *Saturnnguid*· testis· *Nobis* testis· *Guurci*· testis· *Cutulf*· testis··	10	21	62
9	De laicis· *Cinguernn*· testis· *Collbiu*· testis· *Cohorget*· testis· *Ermin*· testis·· *Hourod*· testis·	12	26	73
		22	47	135
	Pars III Sanctio			
10	Quicunque custodierit benedictus erit·	4	14	34
11	et qui franxerit maladictus erit· a Deo··	7	14	32
		11	28	66
		77	144	397

Part I Disposition

1 This writing shows that *Rhys* and *Luith Grethi* gave *Treb Guidauc*

2 *as the historians say.*

3 This is its tribute:

4 *forty loaves and a wether in the summer*

5 *and forty loaves in the winter and a sow*

6 *and forty* [?] *suckling pigs*

7 to God and Saint Teilo.

Part II Attestation

8 God witness, *Saturnnguid* witness, *Nobis* witness, *Guurci* witness, *Cuthwulf* witness.

9 From among laymen: *Cinguernn* witness, *Collbiu* witness, *Cohorget* witness, *Ermin* witness, *Hourod* witness.

Part III Sanction

10 Whoever will have guarded will be blessed.

11 And he who will have broken will be cursed by God.

8 The arrangement of the text and the translation of Latin passages are mine. The translation of Welsh passages is that of Professor Wendy Davies, 'The Latin charter-tradition in western Britain, Brittany and Ireland in the early mediaeval period' in *Ireland in Early Mediaeval Europe, Studies in Memory of Kathleen Hughes*, ed. Dorothy Whitelock, Rosamond McKitterick, David Dumville (Cambridge University Press, 1982), pp. 258–80 at 263 n. 22.

The memorandum, occupying eleven lines, is composed in duple ratio, in multiples of eleven words, the Disposition of forty-four words being followed by the Attestation of half as many words, twenty-two, followed by the Sanction of half as many words, eleven, the whole composition containing seventy-seven words, of which half, thirty-nine, are in Welsh. The total number of syllables is 144, the number of cubits in the walls and part of the number of the elect of the heavenly Jerusalem, as stated in Apocalypse VII 4 and XXI 12.

The seventy-seven words of *Memorandum III* divide by one-ninth at 9, at | *Treb Gujdauc*, the name of the place under consideration, as in *Memorandum II*. The forty-four words of the Disposition divide by one-ninth at 5, at | *Ris et Luith Grethi*, the names of the donors, as in *Memorandum I*.

Three times the tribute is reckoned in units of forty, *douceint*, in the first forty words. From | *hic est census eius* 3 to the end of the Disposition there are forty syllables. From | *douceint torth* 4 to *douceint* | *torth* 5 inclusive there are forty letters.

Reckoning letters as numerals the names *RIS ET LUITH GRETHI* bear a numerical value of 16+9+17+5+18+10+19+9+18+8+7+16+5+18+8+9 or 192, including 1 for a space after each of the four words, 196, which is exactly the number of letters in the Disposition.

IIII. MEMORANDUM V: THE MANUMISSION OF BLEIDIUD AP SULIEN

The text of *Memorandum V* appears in the left and lower margins of page 218.

[Nec]esse est
[scri]bere lit
[eras] quod iiii·^{or} fi
[lii b]ledri· gu
[orti]girnn·
[cim]ulch· et
**** arthuis·
[dede]runt li
[bert]atem ble
[idiud f]ilio sul
[gen e]t semini
[suo] insempi
[tern]um· **P**ro pre
[tio A]tque hoc est
[confirmatio] quod dedit
[pro] liberta
[te ei]us quatuor
[libr]as et oc
[to u]ncias· —

[Coram] idoneis
[his t]estibus· de
[laic]is· **R**iguo
[llau]n filius
[coff]ro· guen
*** fili^{u}s
****r· guoluíc
[filius **]an· **O**v
**** filius guur
[cinn]im· mer
[chgu]inn filius salus· arthan· filius· cimulch· iudri· filius· iudnerth· **D**eclericís vero Nobis episcopus teiliav·
[sat]urnguid sacerdos teiliav· **D**ubrino· et cuhelin· filii episcopis· **S**aturnbiu cam ibiav· et sulgen
[scho]lasticus qui hec fideliter scripsit·· qui custodierit hoc decretvm libertatis bleidiud et prolis eius sit
[bened]ictus· qui autem non custodierit· **S**it maledictus á deo et a teiliav incuius euangelio scriptum est et
[dica]t omnis populus fiat fiat··,

Pars I Dispositio
1 Necesse est scribere literas quod quatuor filii *Blédri·*
Guortigirnn· Cimulch· et **** *Arthuis·*
dederunt libertatem *Bleidiud* filio *Sulgen* et semini súo in sèmpitérnum·
2 **P**ro pretio·
3 Atque hoc est confirmatio quod dedit pro libertate eius quatuor libras et ócto úncias·—
Pars II Attestatio
4 Coram idóneis his téstibus·
5 De laicis·
***R**iguollaun·* filius· *Cóffro·*
*Guen***·* filius· *****r·*
Guoluíc· filius· ***an·*
O**v*·* filius· *Guúrcinnim·*
Merchguinn· filius· *Sálus·*
Arthan· filius· *Címulch·*
Iudri· filius· *Iúdnerth·*
6 **D**e clèricis uéro·
***N**obis·* epíscopus· *Teíliau·*
Saturnguid· sacérdos· *Teíliau·*
***D**ubrino·* et *Cuhelin·* fílii epíscopis·
***S**aturnbiu·*
Camibiau·
et *Sulgen* scholasticus qui hec fidéliter scrípsit·

Pars III Sanctio

7 Qui custodierit hoc decretum libertatis *Bleidiud* et prolis eius sít benedíctus·

8 Qui autem non custodierit· **S**it maledictus à *Deo* et a *Teiliau*· in cuius euangélio scríptum est·

9 et dicat omnis pópulus fiat fiat··,

Part I Disposition

1 It is necessary to write letters that the four sons of *Bledri*,
Vortigern, Cimulch, and ****, *Arthuis*,
gave freedom to *Bleidiud* son of *Sulien* and his seed forever.

2 For a price.

3 And in this is the confirmation that he gave for his freedom four pounds and eight ounces.

Part II Attestation

4 In the presence of these suitable witnesses:

5 From among laymen:
Riguollaun son of *Coffro*,
*Guen**** son of ****r*,
Guoluic son of ****dan*,
*Ou***** son of *Guurcinnim*,
Merchguinn son of *Salus*,
Arthan son of *Cimulch*,
Iudri son of *Iuḍnerth*.

6 From among clerics however:
Nobis bishop of *Teilo*,
Saturnguid priest of *Teilo*,
Dubrino and *Cuhelin* sons to bishops,
Saturnbiu,
Camibiau,
and *Sulien* the scholastic, who wrote these things faithfully.

Part III Sanction

7 He who will have guarded this decree of the freedom of *Bleidiud* and his offspring, may he be blessed.

8 But he who will not have guarded, may he be cursed by *God* and by *Teilo*, in whose Gospel it has been written.

9 And let all the people say, 'Let it be done', 'Let it be done'.

There are three parts of the Disposition, three of the Attestation, and three of the Sanction. There are seven names in the Disposition, seven lay witnesses, and seven clerical witnesses.

The text of the Disposition is confirmed in that the thirty-nine words divide by one-fourth and three-fourths at 10 and 29, at *quatuor* | and | *quatuor*. Between the second *quatuor* and *octo* there are eight letters. The sentence *atque hoc est confirmatio quod dedit pro libertate eius quatuor libras et octo uncias* 'and in this is the confirmation that he gave for his freedom four pounds and eight ounces' means what it says. The price Bleidiud paid, four pounds and eight ounces, amounted, reckoning sixteen ounces to the pound, to seventy-two ounces, confirmed by a sentence that contains seventy-two letters.

There are thirty-three words in the Sanction, eleven in the first sentence and twenty-two in the last two sentences, and seventy-two syllables. The thirty-three words of the Sanction with the thirty-nine words of the Disposition equal 72.

When the text was complete there may have been as many syllables in the Attestation as words in the entire memorandum, 122. Of that number sixty-six words occur between *Sulgen* and *Sulgen*, the name of the writer. Half of that number, thirty-three words, are names.

The 122 words of *Memorandum V* divide by one-ninth at 14, at | *libertatem Bleidiud*, the principal subject of the composition. The thirty-three words of the Sanction divide by one-ninth at 4, at | *libertatis Bleidiud*.

The thirty-nine words of the Disposition divide by 9:8 at 21 and 18, at *Sulgen* |, and the fifty words of the Attestation divide by one-ninth and eight-ninths at 6 and 44, at | *Sulgen*, the name of the writer.

Memorandum V issued probably from the period during which Nobis was *episcopus Teiliau*, before A.D. 893, when in an account of the year 885 Asser wrote of *illud monasterium et parochiam Sancti Degui ... et Nobis archiepiscopum propinquum meum*,[9] before 873, when, according to the *Annales Cambriae, Nobis episcopus et Mouric moriuntur*, before 840, when, according to the same source, *Nobis episcopus in Minius regnauit*.

V. A NARRATIVE LLANCARFAN CHARTER: GUENGARTH TO SAINT CADOG

Late in the eleventh century (*ca* 1095–1104) Lifris of Llancarfan, son of Heruuald Bishop of Llandaff (1056–1107), composed a *Vita Sancti Cadoci*.[10] Analysing the text of London, British Library, MS Cotton Vespasian A.XIV, folios 17r–43v, written about A.D. 1200, Hywel D. Emanuel distinguished the contents of Lifris's original *Vita*, additions made before execution of the Vespasian manuscript, additions made during execution of this manuscript, and additions made after its execution.[11] Among the additions made during execution of this manuscript Emanuel included texts of fourteen charters, §§ 55–68, which must therefore have acquired their present written form not later than the twelfth

9 *Asser's Life of King Alfred together with the Annals of Saint Neots erroneously ascribed to Asser*, edited by William Henry Stevenson, new impression with article on recent work on Asser's Life of Alfred by Dorothy Whitelock (Oxford: Clarendon Press, 1959), § 79 pp. 65–6. Howlett, *Cambro-Latin Compositions*, pp. 84–94.

10 Wade-Evans, *Vitae*, pp. 24–141.

11 Hywel D. Emanuel, 'An Analysis of the Composition of the "Vita Cadoci"', *The National Library of Wales Journal VII* (1951–2), pp. 217–27.

century. In the text of a central eighth charter that follows,[12] capital letters and punctuation marks in boldface represent features of MS Cotton Vespasian A.XIV, folio 40. I have arranged the text in lines and marked the rhythms of the cursus.

I **S**ciendum est quod **M**orcant **R**ex uenando uenit usque ad ripam flúminis **N**ádauon
et iecit accipitrem súper anát*em* **.**
et ambo simul accipiter et anas flumen uolatu tránsmeauérun*t* **.**
II **E**t subito ueniebat **a**quila de ripa maris ut ráperet accípitr*em* **.**
III **Q**uod ut uidit **M**orcant rex : ualde cóntristátus es*t* **.**
IIII **A**st concite alumpnus regis ueniens nomine **G**uengarth **.** eques cum scuto et gladio ac lancea se in flúmen pro*rípuit* **.**
et accipitrem a raptu aquile non modico uiríliter e*rípuit*
uerum etiam leporiter accipitrem cum anate ad manum **M**orcanti **R**ég*is* *átt*ul*it* **.**
illumque tali facinore non minimum létifi*cáuit* **.**
V **Q**uocirca dixit **M**órcant **G**uéngarth*o* **.**
VI **E**cce tribuo tibi uillam **C**adroc in ius héreditárium
habentem longitudinem ab urbe **T**rotguid : usque ad flúmen **N**ádauon **.**
et latitudinem a fonte **G**uengarth **:** usque ad álium fòntem Guéngarth **.**
VII Eodem die **M**orcant et **G**uengarth perrexerunt ad quoddam territórium **C**adóci **.**
et tribuit **G**uengarth Deo et Sancto **C**adoco censum prescripte uille **C**adroc pro anima sua et pro anima **M**órcanti régis **.**
scilicet singulis annis duodecim modios ceruise et sextarium mellis **.** debitum quoque pánem et cárn*em* **.**
VIII **I**nsuper etiam idem **G**uengarth dedit **C**onmogoi Hipiclaur gladium suum deauratum pro anima sua quod habuit pretium septuagínta uaccár*um* **.**
VIIII **Q**ua re consuluit **C**onmogoi **G**uengartho quo gladium illud **M**órcanto prestáre*t* **.**
ut ille donationem **G**uengarthi confirmaret súper pago **C**ádroc
quod et fec*it* **.**
X **Q**ua de re **M**orcant prelibatam donationem rátam hábu*it*
atque scripto corroborauit super manum **S**ulien illam illinc fore liberam et quietam ab omni terreno seruitio **.** uerum funditus obsequio Dei et Sancti Cadóci obnóxia*m* **.**
XI **H**uius réi téstes sun*t* **.**
Morcant super se ipsum **.** ut nullus huius territorii procurator extat nisi Guengarth et héredes illíus **.**
De **C**lericis **. S**ulien **. C**onmogoi **. D**anoc **. G**uorguethen **. L**egan **. E**lgnou **.**
De laicis uero **. G**uingueri **. I**acob **. B**oduan **. E**lguan **. G**urhitr **. C**uncua*n* **.**
XII **Q**uicunque custodierit benedictus erit **.** et qui infregerit maledictus a Déo et à Cadóc*o*
XIII **AME***N* **.**

1 Nadhauon. 5 Marcant. 8 Morcant. 12 Nadauan. 16 .xii.. 17 conmogoy. precium .lxx^{ta}. 18 Conmogoy guengardo. 18 illum. 19 Guengardi. Catroc. 22 illa. obnoxia.

12 Wade-Evans, *Vitae*, § 62 p. 130.

I It is to be known that Morgant the king in hunting came as far as the bank of the river Nadauon,
and he cast a hawk through the air above a duck,
and both together, hawk and duck, passed across the river in flight.

II And suddenly an eagle came from the bank of the sea, that it might seize the hawk.

III Which, as Morgant the king saw, he was greatly saddened.

IIII But a foster son of the king coming quickly, by name Guengarth, a knight, flung himself forth into the river with shield and sword and lance,
and he not a little manfully snatched the hawk from the grasp of the eagle,
but he also graciously brought to the hand of Morgant the king the hawk with the duck,
and by such a deed he made him not a little happy.

V On which account Morgant said to Guengarth,

VI 'Behold, I give to you the town of Cadrog in hereditary right,
having a length from the city Trotguid as far as the river Nadauon,
and a breadth from the well of Guengarth as far as the other well of Guengarth.'

VII On the same day Morgant and Guengarth advanced to a certain territory of Cadog,
and Guengarth gave to God and Saint Cadog a tribute of the forewritten town Cadrog, for his own soul and for the soul of Morgant the king,
that is in individual years twelve measures of beer and a sextarius of honey, bread and meat also owed.

VIII In addition the same Guengarth also gave to Conmogoy for his own soul his own gilded sword Hipiclaur, which had a price of seventy cows.

VIIII For which reason Conmogoy consulted Guengarth that he might present that sword to Morgant,
so that that man might confirm the donation of Guengarth concerning the country of Cadrog,
which he also did.

X By which affair Morgant had the foresaid donation ratified,
and he corroborated in writing on the hand of Sulien that it should in that way be free and quit from all earthly service, but entirely under legal obligation to the service of God and Saint Cadog.

XI Witnesses of this affair are
Morgant for himself, so that there be no procurator of this territory except Guengarth and his heirs,
from among the clerics, Sulien, Conmogoy, Danog, Guorguethen, Legan, Elgnou;
from among the laymen, however, Guingueri, Jacob, Boduan, Elguan, Gurhitr, Cunguan.

XII Whoever may guard [the agreement] will be blessed and who may infringe cursed by God and by Cadog.

XIII Amen.

The author arranged some of his words and ideas in chiastic and parallel patterns.

1	A1	Morcant rex
2	A2	accipitrem super anatem … accipiter et anas
4	A3	et subito ueniebat
4	A4	aquila
4	A5	ut raperet
4	A6	accipitrem
5	A7	quod ut uidit Morcant rex ualde contristatus est
6	A7'	ast concite alumpnus regis ueniens nomine Guengarth eques cum scuto et gladio ac lancea se in flumen proripuit
7	A6'	accipitrem
7	A5'	a raptu
7	A4'	aquile
7	A3'	non modico uiriliter eripuit
8	A2'	accipitrem cum anate
8	A1'	Morcanti regis

10	B1	Morcant
10	B2	Guengartho. ecce tribuo tibi uillam Cadroc in ius hereditariam
13	B3	Guengarth … Guengarth
14	B1	Morcant
15	B3	Guengarth
15	B2	tribuit Guengarth … censum prescripte uille Cadroc
15	B1	Morcanti
17	B3	Guengarth
17	B4	Conmogoi
18	B4	Conmogoi
18	B3	Guengartho
18	B1	Morcanto
19	B2	donationem Guengarthi confirmaret super pago Cadroc
21	B1	Morcant
22	B5	Sulien
24	B1	Morcant
25	B5	Sulien

The author guaranteed the integrity of discrete units of composition with infixed devices. There are, for example, before sentence IV forty-four words, and in sentence IV there are forty-four words.

In sentence VII line 16 in the account of the tribute, *scilicet singulis annis duodecim modios*, the twelfth syllable is the last of *duodecim*, after which there are six syllables before *et sextarium*.

In sentence VIII line 17 *Hipiclaur | gladium suum deauratum pro anima sua quod habuit pretium septuaginta | uaccarum* contains seventy letters and spaces between words.

The author also guaranteed the integrity of the entire composition, which contains thirteen sentences (13 x 1) by naming thirteen witnesses and concluding with a sanction containing thirteen words.

Sentence I contains twenty-six words (13 x 2). From the beginning of the text to the end of the witness list there are twenty-six lines.

The name *Morcant* recurs at multiples of 4. *Morcant* 1 is the fourth word (4 x 1), *Morcant* 5 the fortieth word (4 x 10), *Morcanti* 8 the eightieth word (4 x 20), *Morcant* 10 the twelfth word from that inclusive (4 x 3), *Morcant* 14 the thirty-second word from that inclusive (4 x 8), between which and *Morcanti* 15 there are twenty-four words (4 x 6). After *Morcanto* 19 *Morcant* 20 is the sixteenth word (4 x 4), between which and *Morcant* 24 there are thirty-two words (4 x 8), after which there are forty-four words (4 x 11) to the end of the charter proper at *Cadoco* 26.

Reckoning letters as numerals, the name *MORCANT* bears a numerical value of 11+13+16+3+1+12+18 or 74. From *Morcant rex* | 1 to | *Morcanti* regis 8 there are seventy-four words. From | *Morcanti* 8 to | *Morcant* 10 there are seventy-four letters.

The name *NADAVON* bears a numerical value of 12+1+4+1+19+13+12 or 62. From | *Sciendum est quod Morcant rex uenando uenit ad ripam fluminis Nadauon* to *se in flumen* [*sc. Nadauon*] *proripuit* | 6 there are sixty-two words. In sentence VI line 12 the clause *habentem longitudinem ab urbe Trotguid usque ad flumen Nadauon* contains sixty-two letters and spaces between words.

The name *TROTGUID* bears a numerical value of 18+16+13+18+7+19 +9+4 or 104. There are 104 words before | *Trotguid.*

The name *GUENGARTH* bears a numerical value of 2+19+5+12+7+1+16 +18+8 or 93. Sentence IIII line 6, in which the name first appears, contains ninety-three letters. After the second mention of the name *Guengarth* | 10 the ninety-third word is *Guengartho* | 18. From *Guengarthi* | 20 to the end of the Disposition at *obnoxiam* | 22 there are ninety-three syllables.

The name *CADROC* bears a numerical value of 3+1+4+16+13+3 or 40. Between *uillam Cadroc* | 11 and | *prescripte uille Cadroc* 15 there are forty words.

The name *CONMOGOI* bears a numerical value of 3+13+12+11+13+7 +13+1 or 73. From | *Conmogoi* 19 to *Conmogoi* | 25 inclusive there are seventy-three words. The name *SULIEN* bears a numerical value of 17+19+10+9+5+12 or 72. From *Conmogoi* | 19 to | *Sulien* 22 there are seventy-two syllables. From | *Conmogoi* 19 to *Sulien* | *Conmogoi* 25 *Sulien* is the seventy-second word.

CONCLUSIONS

The memoranda considered above were added to the manuscript of the Gospels of Saint Teilo probably during the two decades between 820 and 840. Given the tightly knit structure of *Memorandum V* the scribe may be presumed to be identical with the composer, justifying addition of Sulien of Llandeilo Fawr to the list of Cambro-Latin writers.

Memoranda I, II, III, and *V* look as if they were written by four different hands. Spellings of *Gelhi* in *I* but *Gelhig* in *II, frangerit* in *II* but *franxerit* in *III,*

Saturnnguid in *III* but *Saturnguid* in *V*, *maladictus* in *II* and *III* but *maledictus* in *V*, imply the existence at Llandeilo Fawr of at least four men who could write in a shared house style of arithmetically informed prose, composing according to the same rules, even the same ratios, and yet exhibiting idiosyncratic features, in play with monolingual and bilingual passages, rhythmical and unrhythmical passages, uniform and varied spellings.

In the memoranda from Llandeilo Fawr and the charter from Llancarfan the numerical values of personal names and place-names fit in varied units of letters and syllables and words woven into prose that is apparently straightforward, at no point arch or stilted or overwrought, at no point drawing attention to itself.

These five Welsh charters, written by five different men in the ninth and the eleventh or twelfth centuries, conform exactly with a mode of thought and composition exhibited in a tradition of Cambro-Latin texts on inscribed stones and in literary manuscripts unbroken from the fifth century to the thirteenth.[13] As nothing in the Welsh charters we have considered suggests influence from England, one suspects that Anglo-Latin diplomatists may have learned some elements of their craft from a Cambro-Latin tradition, older than the seventh-century documents from Kent, but evident only in Welsh documents extant from the ninth century and later. Each of these Cambro-Latin charters in its richly varied idiosyncrasy tells us something about a quality of intellectual life among literate Welshmen that has entirely escaped the notice of modern scholars. The collective testimony of this tiny fraction of extant Welsh charters affords new criteria for students of Cambro-Latin as of Anglo-Latin diplomatic.

13 Howlett, *Book of Letters, passim*; *Celtic Latin Tradition*, pp. 55–66, 72–81, 193–213, 225–7, 233–42, 273–335, 337–42, 346–51, 363–75; *English Origins of Old French Literature*, pp. 36–51; *British Books in Biblical Style*, pp. 365–445; *Cambro-Latin Compositions, passim*.

IIII

A CORNISH CHARTER

I. MAENCHI THE NOBLEMAN TO SAINT HELDENUS

The text of the oldest extant Cornish charter survives in an eighteenth-century transcript of a cartulary of the abbey of Athelney in Somerset, formerly Phillipps MSS 4810–11, later in the possession of David Rogers of the Bodleian Library, Oxford, now at Downside Abbey. It records the gift of Lanlawren (Old Cornish *lann* 'enclosed cemetery' and *louuern* 'fox') during the reign of Æthelstan, between 924 and 939, from the nobleman Maenchi to Saint Heldenus.[1]

Charta Maenchi Comitis
Qui domum Dei aedificat regnum Dei
desiderat. Maenchi Comes filius Pretig-
nor, pro desideratione Regni Caelestis
S. Heldeno[1] dedit Lanlovern in Diocesim
Sempiternam, pro anima sua cum omni ter-
ra sua, & cum coretis[2] omnibus. Hoc fecit
in Saxonia Patria in Insula Adalne,[3] reg-
nante Athelstano Rege in festivitate omniu*m*
Sanctorum[4] ante altare Petri & Pauli, cora*m*
Deo & omnibus Sanctis ejus, coram Seigno
Abbate. Quicunque[5] hoc mutaverit aut p*er*
vim rapuerit, vel ad hoc non consenserit,
Anathema sit de Deo & S. Heldeno,[6] & omnibus Sanctis.

1. Glossed *Athelwino.*
2. Underlined in the manuscript.
3. Glossed Athalny (not *Athalnay* as Bates printed).
4. The MS. reading appears to be *Sanctorun*'
5. *Qui-* is underlined and glossed Cui.
6. Glossed *Athelwino.*

1 Sawyer, *Charters*, no. 1207 p. 353. *BCLL*, no. 164 p. 52. O.J. Padel, 'Two New Pre-Conquest Charters for Cornwall', *Cornish Studies, Journal of the Institute of Cornish Studies VI* (1978), pp. 20–7; 'The Text of the Lanlawren Charter', *Ibid.* VII (1980 for 1979), pp. 43–4.

Let us arrange the text *per cola et commata.*

I	CHARTA MAÉNCHI CÓMI*TIS*	a	3	7	20
II	Qui dom*um* *Dei* aedifi*cat* regn*um* *Déi* desíder*at*.	b	7	17	38
III	Maenchi Comes fílius Pretígnor	c	4	10	27
	pro desideratione régni caelés*tis*	a	4	13	30
	Sancto Heldeno dédit Lanlóuern	d	4	10	27
	in diócesim sèmpitérna*m*	e	3	9	21
	pro ánim*a* *súa*	f	3	6	11
	cum ómni terr*a* *súa*	f	4	7	15
	et cum córetis ómnib*us* .	a	4	8	19
IIII	Hoc fecit in Saxónia pátri*a*	f	5	11	23
	in ínsula Ádaln*e*	g	3	7	14
	regnante Áthelstano Rég*e*	g	3	9	22
	in festiuitate Ómnium Sanctóru*m*	e	4	12	28
	ante altare Pétri et Paúli	h	5	10	22
	coram Deo et ómnibus sànctis eí*us*	a	6	12	28
	coram Seígno Abbát*e* .	g	3	7	17
V	Quicunque hóc mutá*uerit*	b	3	8	21
	aut per uím rap*úerit*	b	4	7	17
	uel ad hoc nón consén*serit*	b	5	8	22
	anáthema sit dé *Deo*	i	4	8	16
	et Sáncto Hél*deno*	i	3	6	15
	et ómnibus sánc*tis* .	a	3	6	16
			87	198	469

I A CHARTER OF MAENCHI THE NOBLEMAN

II He who builds the house of God desires the kingdom of God.

III Maenchi the nobleman, son of Pretignor,
for the sake of desire of the heavenly kingdom
gave to Saint Heldenus Lanlawren
as an eternal possession
for the sake of his own soul
with all its own land
and with all the fishgarths.[2]

2 The word *coretis* from Old Cornish and Old Welsh *cored* 'weir', 'dam', 'fishgarth' affords a rare example of a borrowing from a vernacular into Insular Latin before the

IIII This he did in the fatherland Saxony [*i.e.* Wessex]
in the Isle of Athelney,
with Æthelstan the King reigning,
on the feast of All Saints,
before the altar of Peter and Paul,
in the presence of God and all His saints,
in the presence of Seignus the Abbot.

V Whoever will have changed this
or through force will have seized
or will not have consented to this,
should be anathema by God
and by Saint Heldenus
and by all saints.

There are twenty-two (11 x 2) letters and spaces in the title, the first of twenty-two lines, the last sentence containing twenty-two words, presumably because the drafter of the charter had read that God had created twenty-two things in Genesis I, that there are twenty-two letters in the Hebrew alphabet and twenty-two books in the Hebrew Bible, and twenty-two letters in his Latin alphabet, *ABCDEFGHILMNOPQRSTVXYZ*.

After the title sentence II contains twice twenty-two, forty-four (11 x 4), letters and spaces and seven words, followed by seventy-seven (11 x 7) words, fifty-five (11 x 5) in sentences III and IIII, and twenty-two in sentence V.

After sentence II, which contains seven words, sentence III contains seven lines; sentence IIII contains seven lines; sentence II, which begins *Qui*, and sentence V, which begins *Quicunque*, together contain seven lines.

The title *Charta Maenchi Comitis* and sentence II, which begins *Maenchi Comes*, together contain twenty-nine words.

Sentence II, which begins *Qui*, and sentence V, which begins *Quicunque*, together contain twenty-nine words.

Sentence IIII contains twenty-nine words.

The entire composition contains 555 (111 x 5) letters and spaces. In Roman numerals the number DLV exhibits descending value with omission of the alternate numerals M and C and X and I. From | *Qui domum Dei aedificat to in festiuitate* | *Omnium Sanctorum* there are 305 letters and spaces, exactly the number of days from 1 January to 1 November, All Saints' Day.

In the widely attested earlier form of reckoning letters as numbers,[3] the name *MAENCHI* has a numerical value of 11+1+5+12+3+8+9 or 49. In the

Norman Conquest, after which the practice became more frequent. For other examples see David Howlett and Anthony Harvey, 'An Attack on the Welsh Master Ioruert', *Archivum Latinitatis Medii Aevi* LII (1994), pp. 281–5; Howlett, *Cambro-Latin Compositions*, pp. 96–100; 'A Polyglot Glossary of the Twelfth Century', pp. 87–9.

3 See above, p. 62 n. 5.

words *CHARTA MAENCHI COMITIS Qui domum Dei aedificat regnum Dei desiderat Maenchi Comes filius Pretignor*, among which the name *Maenchi* appears twice, there are ninety-eight (49 x 2) letters and spaces between words.

CONCLUSIONS

The rules of composition of this oldest extant Cornish charter are identical with the rules of composition exhibited both on Cornish Latin inscribed stones and in Cornish Latin literary texts from the beginnings of Latin literacy to the thirteenth century.[4] Comparison with earlier and contemporary charters reveals this document as distinct from English compositions like those considered in chapter II and from Welsh compositions like those considered in chapter III. Our eighteenth-century transcript of Maenchi's donation affords a glimpse of a local Cornish tradition that may have existed long before the tenth-century transaction it commemorates.

4 Charles Thomas, 'Christian Latin Inscriptions from Cornwall in Biblical Style', *Journal of the Royal Institution of Cornwall*, New Series II.II.IV (1997), pp. 42–66, and *The Penzance Market Cross* (Penzance: Penlee House Gallery and Museum, 1999). Howlett, *Celtic Latin Tradition*, pp. 335–7, 375–86.

V

IRISH CHARTERS

I. CALVUS PERENNIS AND BRÍAN BÓRUMA IN 'THE BOOK OF ARMAGH'

In the year 1005 an Irish cleric, describing himself as *Caluus Perennis*, perhaps a translation of the Irish name *Mael Suthain* 'Ever-Tonsured', advanced the metropolitan claims of the church of Armagh in a note added in a larger bolder hand than that of the preceding and following texts to folio 16v of *The Book of Armagh*.[1]

Sánct*us* Patríci*us*	aa	2	6	16
iens ad cael*um* mandáuit totum frúct*um*	bb	6	12	32
laboris súi tam babtísm*i*	cc	4	9	21
tam caus*arum* qu*am* élemoisin*árum*	dd	4	11	28
deferendum esse apostólicae úrbi		4	13	29
quae Scotice nominátur Arddmácha ·		4	11	30
Sic reperi in bebliothéc*is* *Scotórum*	e	5	13	31
Ego scripsi id est Cáluus Perénnis		6	11	29
in conspectu Briain imperatór*is* *Scotórum*	e	5	14	36
et quod scrípsi finíui pro omnibus régibus Macériae		8	18	44
		48	118	296

MS: 1 patrius. 7 bebliot^{h}ics. 10 finituit *with both ts pointed for deletion.*

Saint Patrick
going to heaven commanded the entire fruit
of his labour, as of baptism,
as of legal cases so of alms,
to be brought to the apostolic city

1 *BCLL*, no. 616 p. 158. *The Tripartite Life of Patrick, with Other Documents Relating to that Saint*, ed. Whitley Stokes, Rolls Series LXXXIX (London: HMSO, 1887), vol. II p. 336. *Liber Ardmachanus: The Book of Armagh*, ed. John Gwynn (Dublin: Royal Irish Academy, 1913) f. 16v, p. 32. There is a facsimile of this text as frontispiece. *Book of Armagh, The Patrician Documents*, ed. Edward Gwynn, Facsimiles in Collotype of Irish Manuscripts III (Dublin: Irish Manuscripts Commission, 1937). *The Course of Irish History*, ed. T.W. Moody and F.X. Martin, rev. ed. (Cork: Mercier Press, 1994), ill. 41 p. 109.

which in Irish is named Armagh.
Thus have I discovered in the libraries [or 'Bibles'] of the Irish.
I, that is, 'Ever-Tonsured' [Irish Mael Suthain], have written
in the sight of Brían [Bóruma], Emperor of the Irish,
and what I have written I have completed before all the kings of Maceria.

Here, in a note which may at first seem artless, are ten lines of prose, which divide by extreme and mean ratio at 6 and 4. In *The Book of Armagh* the first of the major six lines and the first of the minor four lines both begin with capital letters *S*. All ten lines end with cursus rhythms. Among the first six lines there is one example of *cursus tardus*, three of *trispondiacus*, and two of *cursus planus*. Among the last four lines there are three examples of *cursus planus* and one of *dispondeus dactylicus*. The first four lines exhibit internal rhyme, and the last six do not. There are twenty-four words in the six-lined major part and twenty-four words in the four-lined minor part. From the beginning to the central word | *Arddmacha* exclusive there are fifty-nine syllables, and from | *Arddmacha* inclusive to the end there are fifty-nine syllables. The central letters, 148th from the beginning and 148th from the end of 296, are in *Arddmacha*.

The golden section of the forty-eight words falls at 30 and 18, at *Ego* |, the thirtieth word. In the eighteen-word minor part the golden section falls at 11 and 7, at the eleventh word from the end, | *Briain*. Between *scripsi* | 8 and *scripsi* | 10 there are eleven words. After *Scotice* | 6 *Scotorum* | 9 is the eighteenth word. Before | *Scotorum* 9 the eleventh word is | *Scotorum* 7. The author refers to himself not only at the golden section, *Ego* | in line 8, but also at eight-ninths of the forty-eight words, which falls at 5 and 43, at *scripsi* | *finiui* in line 10.

In the word *bebliotͱics* the scribe wrote not superscript *h* but Greek *dasia* ͱ, which he might have learned from passages in *The Book of Armagh* written by Ferdomnach (*ob.* 845), who placed it on the line as a letter.[2] If one supposed that the scribe used the character simultaneously to represent asper, the rough breathing of *h*, and the left half of *eta* for *e*,[3] the only error would be reversal of *ic* in *bebliothecis*. By noting further the rhymes in ***in bibliothecis Scotorum*** with those in *Briain* ***imperatoris Scotorum***, one might suppose that the original intention was to write *bibliothecis* in the correct Classical form. The only other uncorrected error in the entire passage would be omission of *ci* from *Patricius*, perhaps a result of nervousness if the scribe was being watched by Brían Bóruma and all the kings of Maceria.

The tradition of reckoning letters as numbers, practised widely among the Welsh and the Cornish from the Romano-British period onward and among the English from the seventh century onward,[4] was practised among early

2 David Howlett, 'Hellenic Learning in Insular Latin', *Peritia* XII (1998), pp. 54–78.

3 For use of ; to represent simultaneously *-us* and punctuation points see Howlett, '*Aldhelmi Carmen Rhythmicum*', p. 120 n. 3.

4 See above, pp. 21, 25, 32, 35, 41, 47, 62, 66, 73, 77–8, and below, pp. 85–6, 91, 94, 99.

Hiberno-Latin authors, notably Bishop Ultán moccu Conchobuir of Ardm-Breccáin (*ob.* 657), who employed the system in the Brigitine hymn *Xpistus in nostra insula.*[5] In this note the nominative forms of the most important names, SANCTUS PATRICIUS and ARDDMACHA and BRIAN bear numerical values of 18+1+13+3+19+20+18 and 15+1+19+17+9+3+9+20+18 and 1+17+4+4+12+1+3+8+1 and 2+17+9+1+13 or 203+51+42 or 296, exactly the number of characters in the composition.

Here in the oldest extant Hiberno-Latin charter we read of an exchange, Brían confirming privileges of Armagh as the metropolitan church of Ireland, the church of Armagh confirming Brían's title as *Imperator Scotorum*, in the most important book in Armagh, in a note composed in self-authenticating form.

II. DIARMAIT MAC MURCHADA AND THE FOUNDATION OF KILLENNY

The Cistercian order was introduced into Ireland by Saint Malachy of Armagh, a friend of and subject of a biography by Saint Bernard of Clairvaux. Between 1162 and 1165 Diarmait Mac Murchada King of Leinster confirmed a grant by Diarmait Ua Riain for the foundation of a Cistercian house at Killenny, record of which survives among muniments of the Marquess of Ormonde, formerly in the Evidence Room of Kilkenny Castle, now Dublin, National Library of Ireland, MS D. 1.[6]

I UNIVERSIS SANCTE MATRIS ECCLÉSIE FÍLI*IS* .
ARCHIEPISCOPIS . EPISCOPIS . **A**BBÁTIBUS . PRESBÍ*TERIS* .
REGIBUS . **D**ÚCIBUS . COMÍT*IBUS* .
ET OMNIBUS TAM LAICIS QUAM CLERICIS IN XPÍSTO **F**IDÉL*IBUS* .
DIARMETIUS NUTU DEI RÉX LAGNÉNS*IUM*
SALUTEM . ET PÁCIS SPÍR*ITUM* .

II **N**otum facimus preséntibus et pós*teris* .
quod nos terram quam Diarmait UaRríain dux Uanróna*i* .
per nóstram licéntia*m* .
in remissionem peccatórum suó*rum*
Felici **a**bbati de Ossarge et omni eiusdem lóci conuéntu*i* .

5 David Howlett, 'The Brigitine hymn *Xpistus in nostra insula*', *Peritia* XII (1998), pp. 79–86.

6 *BCLL*, no. 629 pp. 160–1. 'The Charters of the Cistercian Abbey of Duiske in the County of Kilkenny', ed. Constance Mary Butler and John Henry Bernard, *Proceedings of the Royal Irish Academy* XXXV C (1919–1920), pp. 1–188 at 5–6. John T. Gilbert, *Facsimiles of National Manuscripts of Ireland* (London: HMSO, 1878), Part II pl. LXII. Noel Kissane ed., *Treasures from the National Library of Ireland* (Boyne Valley Honey Company, 1994), pl. 60 p. 136. I owe thanks for helpful criticism to Marie Therese Flanagan.

ad monasterium in honore beatissime Dei genitricis semperque uírginis Maríe .
sanctique Benedicti abbatis tradidit construénd*um* .
confirmá*mus* .
mánutené*mus* .
et nostri sigilli confirmatióne muní*mus* .

III **H**ec ígitur est térr*a* .
monachis iure perpétuo trádit*a* .
Dun-Inni .
Ceall-Mochomoc .
Muleann-Morain .
Ardsem-Dilli .
Bale-O-Chianugain .
Raith-Inphoboil .
Breslach .
Ceall-Nisi .
Bale-meic-Marcaig .
Druim-Ro .
Bale-meic-Laurada .
Bale-O-Gaillin .
Bale-O-Maille .
Leas-meic-Mellelua .
cum omnibus *suis pértinéntiis* .
in aquis . *in* páscuis . *in* síluis .

IIII **N**am Ceall-Lainne cum omnibus **a**dhuc *suis pértinéntiis* .
scilicet **R**aith-Memb*rain* . et Ard-Pet*rain* .
tam in fluminibus quam in prátis et nemórib*us* .
Donatus uenerabilis **L**eth-Glennénsis epíscop*us* .
ad grángiam fáciénda*m* .
sicut melius de nobis habuit perpetualiter cum nóstra licénti*a* .
prefátis mónach*is* .
quibus de sua parrochia in sui presentia predicta *terra*
scilicet **D**un-Ínni et cé*tera* .
fuit dáta trádidit .

V **I**nterdicimus ergo ne **a**liquis hominum de prefatis terris ausu témerário .
ab eisdem monachis et eorum in perpetuum súccessóribus .
nec passum pédum au*férre* .
nec uiolentiam monasterio si ibi fuit uel eius grangiis si hábuit in*férre* .
aut ígnem appón*ere* .
siue aliquid **a**b eis furtim abstrahere presumat [? l. presúmat abstráh*ere*] :
sed omni**a** in pace ecclesie integra et illibáta dimítt*ere* .

VI **Q**uia si quis contra nos in Dei ecclesiam manum forefaciendo audácter porréx*erit* .
res súas si habú*erit* .
uitam si non : irreuocabíliter p*ér*de*t* .

VII **Da**tum **a**pud Belach-Gaurain .
Teste **L**aurentio **D**ubliniensi **A**rchiepiscopo .
Donato **L**eth-Glennensi episcopo .
Felice abbate de Ossarge .
Murchad filio Murchada .
Murcherdach filio eius .
Domnallo Caimanach .
Diarmait UaRriain .
Padin. UaHeda .
Murchad UaBrain .
Dalbach eiusdem filio .
[Dullayng HuaNualla
Diarmayd HuaRya]
et Uonncuan Ua.Diarmada .
et Amleib macCotaltain ;
[Kekach HuaCoscrayg
Kerill macGilla Nanac
Domnall Ruad
Gilla Padrayg HuaInacada
Donchad HuaInedayg
Diarmaid HuaFiachain
Dullayng macLegussa
Florentio regis notario]

8 uarrian. 33 pertinensiis. 36 ardpet^{a}im.

I TO ALL HOLY MOTHER CHURCH'S SONS,
ARCHBISHOPS, BISHOPS, ABBOTS, PRIESTS,
KINGS, DUKES, EARLS,
AND TO ALL FAITHFUL MEN, LAYMEN AS WELL AS CLERICS,
DIARMAIT BY THE APPROVING NOD OF GOD KING OF MEN OF LEINSTER,
[SENDS] GREETING AND THE SPIRIT OF PEACE.

II We make known to present men and to men who come after
that we the land which Diarmait UaRiain Duke of Uanronai
through our licence
for the remission of his own sins
to Felix Abbot of Ossory and the whole convent of the same place

for a monastery in honour of the most blessed begetter of God and ever virgin Mary
and of Saint Benedict the abbot handed over to be constructed
we confirm,
we maintain,
and by confirmation of our seal we fortify.

III This therefore is the land
handed over to the monks in perpetual right:
Dun-Inni,
Ceall-Mochomoc,
Muleann-Morain,
Ardsem-Dilli,
Bale-O-Chianugain,
Raith-Inphoboil,
Breslach,
Ceall-Nisi,
Bale-meic-Marcaig,
Druim-Ro,
Bale-meic-Laurada,
Bale-O-Gaillin,
Bale-O-Maille,
Leas-meic-Mellelua,
with all the things pertaining to it,
in waters, in pastures, in forests.

IIII For Ceall-Lainne with all the things pertaining to it until now,
understand Raith-Membrain and Ard-Petrain,
as well in rivers as in fields and in woods,
Donnchad the venerable Bishop of Leth-Glenn
for making a grange
just as well as he had from us, perpetually, with our licence,
to the foresaid monks,
to whom from his own parish in his own presence the foresaid land,
understand Dun-Inni and the other things,
was given, he handed over.

V Consequently we enjoin that any one among men from the foresaid lands by impetuous boldness
from the same monks and their successors in perpetuity
should not presume either to take away a pace of the feet
and not to take violence in to the monastery, if there was one, or to its granges if it had [any]
or to set fire

or to abstract anything from them by theft,
but to leave all things intact and unimpaired in the peace of the Church.

VI Because if anyone contrary to us against the Church of God should stretch a hand boldly in wrongdoing,
possessions, if he should have his own,
if not, life he will irrevocably lose.

VII Given at Belach-Gaurain.
As witness Laurence Archbishop of Dublin,
Donnchad Bishop of Leth-Glenn,
Felix Abbot of Ossory,
Murchad son of Murchada,
Murcherdach his son,
Domnall Caimanach,
Diarmait UaRiain,
Padin UaHeda,
Murchad UaBrain,
Dalbach son of the same,
[Dullayng HuaNualla,
Diarmayd HuaRya,]
and Uonncuan UaDiarmada,
and Amleib macCotaltain
[Kekach HuaCoscrayg,
Kerill macGilla Nanac,
Domnall Ruad,
Gilla Padrayg HuaInacada,
Donchad HuaInedayg,
Diarmaid HuaFiachain,
Dullayng macLegussa,
Florentius the king's notary].

Let us note first that the six lines of the Salutation introduce a charter of six parts. Reckoned another way, the Salutation is the first of a seven-part charter of seventy-seven lines, fifty-five for the charter and twenty-two for the list of witnesses.

There are thirty words in the Salutation and twice as many, sixty words, in the Attestation, and ten times as many, 300 words in the entire composition.

The name of the king who confirmed the grant, *DIARMETIUS*, bears a numerical value of 4+9+1+16+11+5+18+9+19+17 or 109. The name of the man who granted the land, *DIARMAIT*, bears a numerical value of 4+9+1+16 +11+1+9+18 or 69. The name of the abbot who received the land, *FELIX*, bears a numerical value of 6+5+10+9+20 or 50. The name of the parish in which the land lay, *DUNINNI*, bears a numerical value of 4+19+12+9+12+12 +9 or 77. From *Diarmetius* | *nutu* to *quam* | *Diarmait* , that is from the space after *Diarmetius* exclusive to the space after *Diarmait* inclusive there are 109 letters and spaces between words. From the space before *Notum facimus* to the space after *Diarmait* inclusive there are sixty-nine letters and spaces. From | *Notum facimus* to *Felici* | inclusive there are fifty syllables. From *Hec igitur est terra monachis iure perpetuo tradita* | *Duninni* to *Duninni et cetera fuit data tradidit* | inclusive there are seventy-seven words.

CONCLUSIONS

Every feature in each of these notarial instruments can be illustrated many times over in Hiberno-Latin compositions from the sixth century to the sixteenth. Both documents resemble other Insular Latin documents more nearly than they resemble anything else, but both are distinctively Irish.

VI

SCOTTISH CHARTERS

I. KING MALCOLM III TO THE MONKS OF SAINT CUTHBERT IN DURHAM

The oldest extant Scottish charter is a memorandum of agreement made A.D. 1093 between Malcolm III, Mael Coluim Ceann Mór, Malcolm Canmore and his family and the community of Saint Cuthbert, probably at the instigation of Turgot Prior of Durham.[1] In the text that follows capital letters and punctuation marks in boldface represent features of London, British Library, MS Cotton Domitian A.VII, folio 52v.

I **H**aec est conuentio quam conuentus Sancti Cuthberti **MAL COLMO** regi
Scottorum et **MARGARITAE** reginae **.** filiisque eorum et
filiabus se perpetuo seruáre promísi*t* **.** 1 a

II **S**cilicet ut pro rege et regina dum uiuunt unus cotidie paúper nutri*átur* **.** 2 b
et duo item pauperes in Cena Domini ad comune mandatum pró eis *hàbeántur* **.** 3 b
et una collecta ad letanias et ad míssam *habeátur* **.** 4 b

III **S**ed utrumque in hac et post hanc uitam tam illi quam filii et filiae eorum
participes sint omnium quae fiunt ad seruitium Dei in monasterio Sáncti
C*u*thbért*i* **.** 5 c
missarum uidelicet **.** psalmorum **.** elemosinarum **.** uigiliárum **.** oràti*ónum* **.** 6 d
et quícquid est hui*ú*smod*i* **.** 7 c

IIII **S**ingulariter uero pro rege et regina a die obitus sui in conuentu triginta
plenaria officia mòrtu*órum* **.** 8 d
et cotidie Verba mea fia*nt* **.** 9 e

V **U**nusquisque autem sacerdos triginta missas **.** ceterorum unusquisque
decem psaltéria cánte*nt* **.** 10 e
Anniuersariusque eorum festiue sicut regis Ethelstani singulis ánnis
celebré*tur* **.** 11 b

1 Hec. MARGARITę reginę. 3 cęna dn̄i. 5 utrūq;. filię. quę. 10 cęterorum. .x.

I This is the convention which the convent of Saint Cuthbert promised that it
would keep perpetually for Malcolm King of the Scots and for Queen
Margaret and for their sons and daughters. 1

1 *Liber Vitae Ecclesiae Dunelmensis nec non Obituaria duo eiusdem Ecclesiae*, ed. J. Stevenson, Surtees Society XIII (1841), p. 73. *Liber Vitae Ecclesiae Dunelmensis: A Collotype Facsimile of the Original Manuscript*, ed. A. Hamilton Thompson, Surtees Society CXXXVI (1923), vol. I f. 48v.

II Understand that on the part of the king and queen, while they live, one pauper should be nourished daily, 2
and in the same way two paupers at the Supper of the Lord [*i.e.* the Eucharist on Maundy Thursday] should be maintained on their part at the Common Commandment [*i.e.* the distribution on Maundy Thursday], 3
and one collect at the litanies and at the mass should be maintained. 4

III But both in this and after this life as much they as their sons and daughters should be participants of all those things which may be performed for the service of God in the monastery of Saint Cuthbert, 5
of masses, understand, of psalms, of alms, of vigils, of prayers, 6
and whatever there is of this sort. 7

IIII Separately, in truth, for the king and queen, from the day of their obit, in the convent thirty plenary offices of the dead 8
and daily 'My words' [Psalm V] should be performed. 9

V Each priest, however, should sing thirty masses, and each of the other men ten psalters, 10
and their anniversary should be celebrated festally just as King Æthelstan's in separate years. 11

The composer of this text infixed many indications of integrity in discrete sentences. The second word of the second line of the second sentence is *duo*. The thirty-four words of sentence II divide by sesquialter ratio 1½:1 or 3:2 at 20 and 14, at *duo* | . The first fourteen words divide by the same ratio at 8 and 6, at | *unum*. The last twenty words divide by the same ratio at 12 and 8, at | *una*. There are eight words between *habeantur* and *habeatur*. The thirty-four words divide by sesquioctave ratio 9:8 at 18 and 16, at the sixteenth word, *duo item pauperes* | . Those sixteen words divide by the same ratio at | *unus cotidie pauper*.

In sentence V line 10, stipulating that each priest should sing ten psalters, contains ten words. The same line, stipulating that each priest should sing thirty masses, contains thirty syllables.

The composer also infixed many indications of integrity in the complete composition, arranging five sentences, I, II, III, IIII, V, and five rhymes, abcde, in eleven lines of text (11 x 1). The heading in sentence I contains twenty-two words (11 x 2). The rest of the text in sentences II–V contains 111 words. Sentence I contains 133 letters, the number of words in the entire text. Sentence V, stating that *Anniuersariusque eorum festiue sicut regis Ethelstani singulis annis celebretur*, concludes a composition that contains 894 letters and spaces, coincident, perhaps, with the year of Æthelstan's birth, A.D 894.[2]

2 As in *Gesta Regum Anglorum* II § 133 William of Malmesbury referred more than thirty years later than this document to Æthelstan's *tricennalis aetas* at his accession, probably in the summer of 924, our author may have reckoned Æthelstan to have been born in 894. See Howlett, *British Books in Biblical Style*, pp. 496, 537–40.

II. KING DUNCAN II TO THE MONKS OF SAINT CUTHBERT IN DURHAM

Let us consider the oldest extant royal Scottish charter of a grant of land that has any claim to authenticity.[3] Although it offers to the diplomatic scholar some apparent difficulties because of the form of the seal, the style of the figure on it, and the manner of its attachment to the charter, Archibald Duncan has presented convincing explanations for all of these. The grant is likely to have been made after the death of Fothad II Bishop of Saint Andrews in A.D. 1093. The charter was written between the death of Malcolm III on 13 November 1093 and the death of Duncan II, Donnchad, on 12 November 1094, probably before the end of the first reign of Donaldbane, Domnall Bán, in May 1094, probably at the instigation of Turgot Prior of Durham. For present purposes the reality of the grant and the authenticity of the charter matter less than its existence as a literary artefact.

In the text that follows capital letters and punctuation marks in boldface represent features of Durham, Dean and Chapter, Miscellaneous Charter 554. I have arranged the text in sentences and marked the rhythms of the cursus.

I **E**go Dunecanus filius regis **M**alcolumb constans hereditárie rex Scótiae **:** dedi in elemosina **S**ancto **C**uthberto et suis seruitoribus **T**ininge ham **. A**lde ham **. S**cuc hale **.** **C**nolle **.** **H**ather uuich **.** et de **B**rocces muthe omne seruitium quod inde habuit **F**ódanus epíscopus **.** et haec dedi in tali quitantia cum sáca et sóca **.** qualem unquam meliorem habuit Sánctus **C**uthbértus **.** ab illis de quibus tenet suas élemósinas **.**

II **E**t hoc dédi pro me ípso **.** et pro ánima pàtris méi **.** et pro frátribus méis **.** et pró uxore méa **.** et pro infántibus méis **.**

III **E**t quoniam uolui quod istud donum stábile ésset **.** Sáncto Cuthbérto **:** feci quod fratres méi concessérunt **.**

IIII **Q**ui autem istud uolúerit destrúere **.** uel ministris Sancti Cuthberti aliquid índe aufèrre **:** maledíctionem Déi **.** et Sáncti **C**uthbérti **.** et méam **:** hábeat **.** Amen

3 *BCLL*, no. 1049 p. 292. J. Anderson, *Selectus Diplomatum et Numismatum Scotiae Thesaurus* (Edinburgh: Thomas and Walter Ruddiman, 1739), pl. IV. J. Raine, *The History and Antiquities of North Durham* (London: John Bowyer Nichols and Son, 1852), app. no. I p. 1, facsimile opp. p. 373. Cosmo Innes and Sir Henry James, *Facsimiles of the National Manuscripts of Scotland* (Southampton: Ordnance Survey, 1867), vol. I pl. II. *Early Scottish Charters Prior to A.D 1153*, ed. Sir Archibald C. Lawrie (Glasgow: James MacLehose and Sons, 1905), no. XII pp. 10, 240–3. P. Hume Brown, *History of Scotland to the Present Time*, 3 vols (Cambridge University Press, 1911), vol. I pl. XIV. A.A.M. Duncan, 'The Earliest Scottish Charters', *The Scottish Historical Review* XXXVII (1958), pp. 103–35.

Crux Dun + ecani Regis Scribtoris Gr + entonis Ace + ard Ul + f Malcolumb
Eadgari + +
Vui + get Her + mer Hem + ming Ælf + ric Teo + dbold Ea + rnulf

I I, Duncan, son of King Malcolm, established King of Scotland by heredity, have given in alms to Saint Cuthbert and his own servants Tyningham, Aldeham, Scuchale, Cnolle, Hatherwick, and of Broxmouth all the service that Bishop Fothad had from that place, and I have given these in such quittance with sake and soke [*i.e.* jurisdiction and the profits that accrue from jurisdiction] as better than Saint Cuthbert ever had from those [lands] from which he holds his own alms.

II And I have given this for myself and for the soul of my father and for my brothers and for my wife and for my infants.

III And as I have wished that that gift to Saint Cuthbert be stable I have made that my brothers have conceded.

IIII Who, however, might wish to destroy that or to take away anything from that place from the ministers of Saint Cuthbert should have the curse of God and Saint Cuthbert and mine. Amen.

The Cross of Dun+can the King, of the scribe Gr+ento, Ace+ard, Ul+f, Malcolm +, of Edgar +, Vui+get, Her+mer, Hem+ming, Ælf+ric, Teo+dbold, A+rnulf.

The scribe of the original charter signed himself as Grento. The scribe of this copy of the charter 'is also to be found at work in one writ of Rufus and two literary manuscripts, and … his name was William. He certainly worked at Durham, and was probably a monk-chaplain.'[4]

The point of the charter is stated in the central word *elemosinas* at the end of the first sentence, the sixtieth of 119 words of the charter proper. The charter contains four sentences, the first two beginning *Ego … dedi … et haec dedi* and *Et hoc dedi*, the last two beginning *Et quoniam uolui* and *Qui autem uoluerit*. The entire text is composed on multiples of the number 4.[5] From the beginning of the charter to | *Sancto Cuthberto* there are twelve words (4 x 3). From | *Cuthberto* to *Cuthbertus* | inclusive there are forty words (4 x 10), and from *Sanctus Cuthbertus* | to *Sancto Cuthberto* | there are also forty words. From | *Sancto Cuthberto* to *Sancti Cuthberti* | there are sixteen words (4 x 4). From *Sancti Cuthberti* | to *Sancti Cuthberti* | there are eight words (4 x 2), after which there are four words (4 x 1) to the end of the text. From *regis* | to *rex* | there are four words (4 x 1). From *istud* | to | *istud* there are twelve words (4 x 3). From | *seruitoribus* to *seruitium* | there are sixteen words (4 x 4). From *uolui* | to *uoluisset* | there are sixteen words. From *elemosina* | to *elemosinas* | there are forty-eight

4 Duncan, 'Charters', p. 122.
5 For other examples of composition on multiples of 4 see below, pp. 91–3, and Howlett, *Caledonian Craftsmanship*.

words (4 x 12). Between the first *dedi* and the third *dedi* there are fifty-two words (4 x 13), and from the first *dedi* to the second *dedi* inclusive there are twenty-four words (4 x 6). There are twelve signatories (4 x 3) to the charter.

Reckoning the elements of the place-names and separated personal names separately, there are 144 words in the entire composition, 144 being the square of 12 and the twelfth number in the Fibonacci series 1–1–2–3–5–8–13–21–34–55–89–144, the number of cubits in the walls of the heavenly Jerusalem and part of the number of the elect.[6] As a device for fixing the date this might suggest the 144th day of the year, 24 May, which fell in the year 1094 on the Wednesday before Whitsun, consistent with 'the period before the end of the first "usurpation" of Donaldbane in May'.[7] There are 888 characters and spaces between words, the value in Greek alphabetic numerical notation of the name IHCOYC being 10+8+200+70+400+200 or 888.[8]

III. KING DAVID I TO ROBERT DE BRUS

A charter from King David I to Robert de Brus, issued at Scone A.D 1124, survives in London, British Library, Cotton Charter XVIII.45.[9]

I.	**DAUID.**		1	2	5
	Dei grátia **R**èx Scottórum .		4	9	21
	Omnibus **B**arónibus súis . et Homínibus . èt Amícis :				
	Fráncis et **Á**nglis :		10	23	54
	Salútem .		1	3	7
			16	37	87
II	**S**ciatis me dedísse . et còncessísse .	5	5	12	29
	Roberto de **B**rus		3	5	13
	Estra Hanent .		2	4	11

6 Apocalypse VII 4 and XXI 12. For other examples of play with the number 144 see above, pp. 35–5, 64–6, and Howlett, 'Five Experiments', pp. 17, 47, 'Seven Studies', pp. 53, *Celtic Latin Tradition*, pp. 21, 25, 264, *British Books in Biblical Style*, pp. 19, 26, *Cambro-Latin Compositions*, pp. 133–4, 137.

7 For other examples of infixed dates see above, pp. 21, 35, 47, 55, and below, p. 93, and Howlett, *Celtic Latin Tradition*, pp. 101–2, 124–9, 152, 187–93, 222–3, 268–73, 332–3, 'Five Experiments', pp. 29–30, 'Seven Studies', pp. 1–6, 20, 68–9, 'A Possible Date for Aldhelm's letter to Heahfrith', *Archivum Latinitatis Medii Aevi* LIV (1996), pp. 99–103, 'Arithmetic Rhythms in Latin Letters', p. 216, 'Numerical Play in Wulfstan's Verse and Prose', pp. 61–7, *Cambro-Latin Compositions*, pp. 42–3, 67–8, 93–4, 107, 126, 140–1, 152.

8 For other examples of play with the number 888 by Insular authors see Howlett, 'Five Experiments', p. 30, *Celtic Latin Tradition*, p. 151, *British Books in Biblical Style*, pp. 119–21, 540, *Cambro-Latin Compositions*, p. 82.

9 Lawrie, *Charters*, no. 54 pp. 48–9. For a facsimile see G.W.S. Barrow, *Scotland and its Neighbours in the Middle Ages* (London: Hambledon, 1992), pl. 1a opp. p. 94.

	et totam terram	3	5	13
	A diuisa **D**unegal de Stra Nit	6	10	23
	usque ad **d**iuisam **R**andúlfi **M**eschíni .	5	12	30
		24	48	119
III	**E**t uólo et concédo .	4	7	15
	ut illam terram .	3	5	13
	et súum castèllum	3	6	15
	béne .	1	2	4
	et hónorífice .	2	6	12
	cum omnibus consuetudínibus súis	4	12	29
	téneat .	1	3	6
	et hábeat .	2	4	8
	uidelicet cum omnibus illis cónsuetudínibus	5	16	39
	quas **R**andulfus **M**eschinus unquam hábuit **in** **C**árduilla .	7	16	45
	et in terra súa de **C**ùmber lánda	7	11	25
	illo die in quo únquam melióres . et liberióres hábuit .	9	21	44
		48	109	255
IIII	Testibus .	1	3	8
	Eustachio filio **I**ohannis .	3	10	22
	et **H**ugone de **M**aruilla .	4	8	18
	et **A**lano de **P**erci .	4	7	14
	et **W**illelmo de **S**umeruilla .	4	9	22
	et **B**erengario **E**nganio .	3	10	19
	et **R**andulfo de **S**ules .	4	7	17
	et **W**illelmo de **M**oruilla .	4	8	20
	et **H**erui filio **W**arini .	4	9	18
	et **E**dmundo **C**amerario .	3	9	18
	Apud **S**conam .	2	4	10
		36	84	186

I David,
by the grace of God King of the Scots
to all his own barons and men and friends French and English,
greeting.

II You should know me to have given and to have conceded
to Robert de Brus
Strath Annan
and all the land
from the boundary of Dúngal of Strath Nith
as far as the boundary of Randolf Meschin.

III And I will and concede
that that land
and its own castle
well
and honourably
with all its own customs,
he should hold
and have,
understand, with all those customs
which Randolf Meschin ever had in Carlisle
and in his own land of Cumberland
on that day on which he ever had them better [*i.e.* 'best'] and freer [*i.e.* 'freest'].

IIII As witnesses:
Eustace son of John
and Hugh de Morville
and Alan de Percy
and William de Somerville
and Berengar Enganius
and Randolph de Sules
and William de Morville
and Harvey son of Warren
and Edmund the Chamberlain.
At Scone.

The charter is composed on multiples of the number 4.[10] There are four parts: I salutation, II the grant with the name of the recipient and details of boundaries, III the terms of the benefaction, IIII the attestation, list of witnesses and location of the act. In I there are sixteen words (4 x 4) and four lines, in II twenty-four words (4 x 6) and six lines, in III forty-eight words (4 x 12) and twelve lines, in IIII thirty-six words (4 x 9) and nine witnesses.

Parts II and III, the grant and the terms of the benefaction, contain twice as many words as part IIII, the attestation, seventy-two to thirty-six. Parts II and III also contain twice as many letters and spaces between words as part IIII, 445 to 222.

The twenty-four words in part II may represent hours in a day. The sixteen words in part I and the thirty-six words in part IIII, together fifty-two, may represent weeks in a year. The 124 words in the entire composition may represent A.D 1124, the year of the grant.[11]

10 See above, pp. 89–91.
11 See above, p. 91 n. 7.

Reckoning letters as numerals the name *DAVID* has a numerical value of 4+1+19+9+4 or 37, exactly the number of syllables in David's salutation in part I. The name *ROBERTUS DE BRUS* has a numerical value of 16+13+2+5+16+18+19+17+4+5+2+16+19+17 or 146. After *Dauid* in the text | *Dei gratia Rex Scottorum omnibus baronibus suis et hominibus et amicis Francis et Anglis salutem Sciatis me dedisse et concessisse Roberto de Brus* | there are exactly 146 letters and spaces between words.

In the text

> .Dauid Dei gratia Rex Scottorum Omnibus Baronibus suis et Hominibus et Amicis Francis et Anglis Salutem. Sciatis me dedisse et concessisse Roberto de Brus Estra Hanent et totam terram a diuisa Dunegal de Stra Nit usque ad diuisam Randulfi Meschini. Et uolo et concedo ut illam terram et suum castellum bene et honorifice cum omnibus consuetudinibus suis teneat et habeat uidelicet cum omnibus illis consuetudinibus quas Randulfus Meschinus unquam habuit in Carduilla et in terra sua de Cumber landa illo die in quo unquam meliores et liberiores habuit. Testibus. Eustachio filio Iohannis et Hugone de Moruilla et Alano de Perci et Willelmo de Sumeruilla et Berengario Enganio et Randulfo de Sules et Willelmo de Moruilla et Herui filio Warini et Edmundo Camerario. Apud Sconam.

there are 777 letters and points and spaces between words.[12] Including all the features marked in boldface above there are exactly 800 letters and points and spaces between words, the number 800 representing perfection.[13]

CONCLUSIONS

All three of these notarial instruments exhibit the conventions of English diplomatic traditions, mediated through Turgot Prior of Durham and the scribes of his house, but applied to the purposes of distinctively styled Scottish kings.

12 For recurrence of the number 777 in twelfth-century Scottish Latin historical and hagiographic compositions see Howlett, *Caledonian Craftsmanship*.

13 Howlett, *British Books in Biblical Style*, pp. 119–24.

VII

A HEBRIDEAN CHARTER

I. REGINALD LORD OF INCHE GAL TO THE ABBEY OF PAISLEY

The oldest extant charter of a Lord of the Isles, a late-twelfth-century grant from Raghnall mac Shomhairle, Reginald son of Somerled Lord of Inche Gal, to the Cluniac abbey of Paisley, survives in a notarial instrument of 9 October 1426.[1] Capital letters and punctuation marks in boldface represent features of Edinburgh, National Library of Scotland, MS Advocates' 34.4.14, folios 104r–105r.

I INSTRUMENTUM DE DENARIIS QUOS DOMINUS DE **I**NCHE GALD DEDIT /
DE OMNIBUS DOMIBUS IN TERRIS SUIS UNDE FUMUS EXIT **.**

II IN DEI NOMINE **A**MEN

III

1 Per hoc presens publicum instrumentum cunctis pateat euidenter quod **a**nno ab incarnatione Domini **M**illesimo quadringentesimo uicesimo sexto mensis uero Octobris die nona / **I**ndictione quinta pontificatus sanctissimi in Xpisto patris et domini domini nostri **M**artini diuina prouidentia pape quinte anno nono / **I**n mei notarii publici ac subscriptorum testium presentia personaliter constitutus **R**eligiosus uir dominus **A**ndreas **S**tuart prior conuentualis monasterii de Passelet / michi subscripto notario presentauit **.** quandam litteram in pargameno scriptam perlegendam et diligenter examinandam ac sub publica forma fideliter copiandam cuius quidem littere tenor sequitur et est talis /

IIII

2 **S**ciant omnes tam presentes quam futuri quod ego Reginaldus filius Sumerled dominus de **I**nche Gal factus sum frater et uxor mea Fonia soror in capitulo domus de Passelet et in toto ordine Cluniacensi /

3 **E**t ego uerus frater et bonus amicus predictis monachis fratribus meis de Passelet in perpetuum mansurus cum heredibus meis et hominibus meis testimonio sigilli mei concessi eiis me daturum sibi pro salute mea et uxoris mee et heredum meorum et hominum in hoc anno octo boues et duos denarios ex qualibet domo unde fumus exit /

4 **E**t post hunc annum singulis annis unum denarium ex qualibet domo tocius terre mee unde fumus exit dabo illis et post me heredes mei dabunt aut maledictionem meam habebunt nisi promptissime dederint /

1 *BCLL*, no. 1169 p. 309. *Registrum Monasterii de Passelet*, ed. Cosmo Innes, Maitland Club (Edinburgh, 1832), pp. 147–9.

V

5 **P**reterea uxor mea domina Fonia concessit eiis se daturam illis in elemosinam decimam omnium rerum que sibi Deus dederit scilicet tam ex ipsis que apud se retinere uoluerit quam ex illis que per terram uel per mare ad uendendum in perpetuum miserit /

VI

6 **E**t quia ego et heredes mei participes sumus et in perpetuum erimus omnium bonorum que in domo de Passelet et in toto ordine fiunt uel in perpetuum fient tam in orationibus quam in ceteris diuine seruitutis obsequiis dedi eiis et concessi et hoc presenti scripto auctoritate sigilli mei roborato confirmaui firmam pacem meam et omnium heredum meorum et hominum cum manutenemento bone fraternitatis ubicunque ipsi uel homines eorum fuerint aut uenerint in terra uel in mari supplicans amicis meis et precipiens omnibus hominibus meis ut ubicunque inuenerint predictos monachos fratres meos aut eorum homines ipsos manuteneant et in suis auxilientur negociis scientes pro certo quod per Sanctum **C**olumbam si aliquis heredum meorum eiis malefecerit maledictionem meam habebit uel si quid mali forte ab hominibus meis uel ab aliis de quibus eos uindicare potero sibi uel suis factum fuerit mortis pena punientur /

VII

7 **H**iis testibus /
Ameleo filio Gil Colmi /
Gil Colmo filio Gil Michael /
Mauricio capellano meo et multis aliis ibi tunc presentibus /

VIII

8 **P**ost quedam littere lecturam et diligentem inspecturam / supplicatum fuit michi per predictum uirum religiosum quatenus eam transcriberem et sub forma publica redigerem /

9 **A**cta fuerunt hec in monasterio predicto de Passelet hora quasi decima ante meridiem /
Anno die mense indictione et pontificatu quibus supra
presentibus prouidis et discretis uiris
dominis Vilelmo Mak / Gilberto de Drumry / **W**ilelmo de Lynn
presbiteris / **W**ilelmo **W**ischart et **J**ohanne Belhous'
cum multis aliis testibus ad premissa uocatis specialiter et rogatis / ..

VIIII

10 **E**t ego **R**obertus de Hopprew presbiter Glasguensis diocesis publicus apostolica auctoritate notarius quia suprascriptam litteram originalem in pargameno scriptam in manu mea tenui et palpaui ac de uerbo in uerbum legi et diligenter examinaui non rasam non abolitam non cancellatam non uiciatam non suspectam sed omni prorsus uicio et suspitione carentem sigillatam quantum michi aparuit uero et indubitato sigillo quondam Reginaldi filii Sumerled domini Inche Gal in cera alba impresso in cuius sigilli medio ex una parte sculpta fuit / una nauis plena hominibus armorum et ex alia parte ymago hominis armati sedentis super equum cum gladio uibrato in manu sua /

11 Ideo de uerbo in uerbum illam per alium michi fidum transcribi feci et copiari et collatione facta cum presenti transsumpto ad litteras originales nullam reperi

discordantiam seu discrepantiam que in aliquo mutare aut ualere poterit intellectum

12 Ideo hic me mea propria manu subscripsi signumque meum solitum et consuetum apposui in fidem et testimonium ueritatis omnium et singulorum premissorum rogatus pariter et requisitus .

3, 5, 6 imperpetuum. 6 *for* manuteneant MS manutenemento. male. 8 delegentem. presbeteris. 10 impressa. 12 appositum. requesitus.

I AN INSTRUMENT CONCERNING PENCE WHICH THE LORD OF INCHE GAL GAVE
FROM ALL THE HOUSES IN HIS OWN LANDS WHENCE SMOKE EXITS.

II IN GOD'S NAME AMEN.

III

1 Through this present public instrument it should be open evidently to all that in the year from the Incarnation of the Lord the thousandth, four-hundredth, twentieth, sixth, on the ninth day, in truth, of the month of October, in the fifth indiction of the pontificate of the most holy father and lord in Christ, our lord by divine providence Pope Martin the Fifth, in the ninth year of my status as public notary, and in the presence in person of the underwritten witnesses, the religious man, lord Andrew Stuart, established prior of the conventual monastery of Paisley, presented to me the underwritten notary a certain letter written on parchment, to be read through and diligently examined and copied faithfully under the form of a public instrument, the tenor of which letter indeed follows, and it is thus.

IIII

2 Let all men know, as much present as future, that I, Reginald son of Sumerled, Lord of Inche Gal, have been made a brother and my wife Fonia a sister in the chapter of the house of Paisley and in the whole Cluniac order.

3 And I, bound to remain in perpetuity a true brother and good friend to the foresaid monks, my brothers of Paisley, with my heirs and my men, under the testimony of my seal I have conceded to them that I will give to them for my salvation and my wife's and my heirs' and men's in this year eight cows and two pence from each house whence smoke exits.

4 And after this year in individual years one penny from each house of my whole land whence smoke exits I will give to them, and after me my heirs will give, or they will have my curse unless they will have given most promptly.

V

5 Besides, my wife, the Lady Fonia, has conceded to them that she will give to them in alms a tenth of all the things which God will have given to her, understand, as much from those things which she will have wished to retain with her, as from those things which she will have sent in perpetuity for selling through the land or through the sea.

VI

6 And because I and my heirs are and will be in perpetuity sharers of all the good things which in the house of Paisley and in the whole order are done or will be done in perpetuity, as much in prayers as in other observances of divine service, I have given to them and conceded and in this present script,

corroborated by the authority of my seal, confirmed my firm peace and all my heirs' and men's with maintenance of good brotherhood, wherever they or their men may be or come on the land or on the sea, beseeching my friends and ordering all my men that wherever they may find the foresaid monks, my brothers, or their men, that they maintain and aid them in their businesses, knowing for certain that, through Saint Columba, if any of my heirs should do ill to them he will have my curse, or if anything of evil will have been done by chance to them or theirs by my men or by others on whom I could avenge them, they will be punished with the penalty of death.

VII

7 With these witnesses:
Ameleus son of Gil Colm,
Gil Colm son of Gil Michael,
Maurice my chaplain and many others there present then.

VIII

8 After the reading and diligent inspection of which letter it was besought to me by the foresaid religious man that I should transcribe and return it under the form of a public instrument.

9 These things were done in the foresaid monastery of Paisley, in about the tenth hour, before midday, in which year, day, month, indiction, and pontificate [stated] above, being present provident and discreet men:
the lords William Mak, Gilbert of Drumry, William of Lynn;
the priests William Wischart and John Belhouse;
with many other witnesses called and asked specially to the prefixed [matters].

VIIII

10 And I, Robert of Hopprew, priest of the diocese of Glasgow, public notary by apostolic authority, because the abovewritten original letter written on parchment I have held in my hand and stroked and from word to word read and diligently examined, not erased, not effaced, not cancelled, not vitiated, not suspect, but lacking indeed every vice and suspicion, sealed, as it appeared to me, with a true and undoubted seal, once Reginald's, son of Sumerled, Lord of Inche Gal, impressed in white wax, in the middle of which seal on one side was sculpted a ship filled with armed men and on the other side the image of an armed man sitting on a horse with a sword brandished in his hand.

11 Therefore from word to word faithful according to the other I made it to be transcribed and copied for myself, and with collation made with the present copy gone over in comparison with the original letters, I found no discordance or discrepancy which could in any matter change or affect the sense.

12 Therefore asked and equally required here I have subscribed myself with my own hand and my accustomed and habitual sign I have affixed for faith and witness of the truth of all and singular prefixed [matters].

Let us begin with the copy of the original charter, the parts here numbered IIII, V, VI, and VII.

The 120 words of part IIII divide by symmetry at 60 and 60, at *concessi eis* | *me daturum*. The 120 words divide by duple ratio 2:1 at 80 and 40, at | *duos denarios.* The 120 words divide by extreme and mean ratio at 74 and 46. The forty-sixth word is *Passelet.* The first forty-six words divide by extreme and mean ratio at 28 and 18. The twenty-eighth word is *Passelet.* The first twenty-eight words divide by extreme and mean ratio at 17 and 11, at references to the donor, *Reginaldus filius Sumerled* | *dominus de Inche Gal* and *factus sum* | *frater.* The last seventy-four words divide by extreme and mean ratio at 46 and 28, at references to time, | *in hoc anno* and *et post hunc annum* | *singulis annis.* Of those the first twenty-eight words divide by the same ratio at 17 and 11, at *sigilli* | *mei* and | *pro salute mea.* The donor's name is the ninth word, *Reginaldus.* The 120 words divide by one-ninth and eight-ninths at 13 and 107. There are thirteen words in *ego* | *Reginaldus filius Sumerled dominus de Inche Gal factus sum frater et uxor mea* | *Fonia.* Reginald's wife's name *FONIA* bears a numerical value of 6+13+12+9+1 or 41. There are forty-one syllables before *Fonia.* In paragraph V about Fonia's donation there are forty-one words from *Preterea* | *uxor mea domina Fonia* to *in perpetuum miserit* |.

As paragraph IIII contains 120 words, paragraph V forty-two words, paragraph VI 141 words, and paragraph VII twenty words, the original charter contains 303 (CCCIII) words, with twenty words naming the witnesses, together 323 (CCCXXIII) words, of which the central 162nd word is the last of Fonia's donation.

Having observed that the donor's name was the ninth word of the original charter, the scribe began in the very heading as he meant to go on, making part I of this nine-part composition, the title, contain nine words in each line, together eighteen (9 x 2), and twice as many syllables, thirty-six (9 x 4), eighteen in each line, and 108 (9 x 12) letters and spaces between words.

In part II he wrote *IN DEI NOMINE AMEN*, containing four words (4 x 1), twice as many syllables, eight (4 x 2), and five times as many letters and spaces, twenty (4 x 5), from the space before *in* to the space after *amen* inclusive.

In part III he wrote nine words before the beginning of the date, which he fixed as *Octobris die* ***nona***, *anno* ***nono*** *in mei notarii publici*, the last word of his preliminaries being the ninety-ninth (9 x 11) before the beginning of the original charter. As the word *Passelet* is twenty-eighth from the beginning of paragraph IIII, the scribe made *Passelet* the twenty-eighth word from the end of paragraph III.

In part VIII there are ten words in the sentence before | *decima* and twelve words before | *meridiem*, this last being the ninth word from the end of the sentence written on 9 October.

In part VIIII the 162 (9 x 18) words of the final paragraph divide by extreme and mean ratio at 100 and 62, at the juncture between the end of description of the seal and the scribe's reference to himself, *in manu sua* | *ideo de uerbo in uerbum illam per alium michi fidum transcribi feci.* The one hundred words of the major part divide by the same ratio at 62 and 38, at the name of the donor, *Reginaldi filii* | *Sumerled.* The sixty-two words of the minor part divide by the same ratio at the scribe's reference to himself, | *me mea propria manu subscripsi.* The description of the seal occupies forty-two words from | *sigillo quondam Reginaldi filii Sumerled* to *in manu sua* | inclusive, which divide by extreme and mean ratio at 26 and 16, at the sixteenth word, *medio* |, so that the golden mean of the passage falls at the word 'mean'.[2] The last twenty-six words of description of the seal divide by the same ratio at 16 and 10, at | *ex una parte*, describing one side in ten words, and | *et ex alia parte*, describing the other side in sixteen words.

Around the central parts, IIII, V, VI, and VII, the copy of Reginald's original charter, the preceding and following notarial paragraphs, parts III and VIII, contain eighty-seven and seventy-three words, together 160 words, with which compare the 162 words of parts III and V, Reginald's and Fonia's donations, and the 162 words of part VIIII, the final scribal paragraph.

All three notarial and scribal parts, III, VIII, and VIIII, contain 87+73+162 or 322 words, with which compare the 323 (CCCXXIII) words of parts IIII, V, VI, and VII, Reginald's original charter.

The 667 letters and spaces of part III, the first notarial paragraph, equal the 667 words of the entire composition.

The total of 667 words avoids, for obvious reasons, equality with the number of the beast, 666. In other respects the composition conforms with the precept of the *Rhetorica ad Herennium* IV XX 27–8, that in composing in apparent, as distinct from actual, equality, one's sums may depart from absolute equality by one or two,[3] the 160 words of the notarial paragraphs differing from the final scribal paragraph of 162 words by 2, and the 322 words of notarial and scribal paragraphs differing from Reginald's original charter of 323 words by 1.

CONCLUSIONS

Robertus de Hopprew shows us punctiliously and elegantly, without a trace of self-importance or pedantry, that he understood perfectly the mind of a professional colleague separated from him by more than two centuries. That twelfth-century colleague shows us with comparable punctilio and elegance that he belonged to a self-conscious tradition of Insular diplomatic that was, even in his day, more than half a millennium old.

2 For other examples of play on *medium* as 'mean' see Howlett, '*Vita I Sanctae Brigitae*', pp. 1–23.

3 Howlett, *Celtic Latin Tradition*, pp. 23–6, and *British Books in Biblical Style*, pp. 24–7.

EPILOGUE

Recently Roger Tomlin edited a text from a wooden writing tablet from the Walbrook in London, datable to 14 March 118, dealing with disputed ownership of a five-acre wood in Roman Kent.[1] No one would suppose that the seventh-century Kentish charters with which we began this study derive directly from that Romano-British document. But one can infer reasonably from the literary tradition of the fifth-century Romano-Britons Pelagius, Saint Patrick, and Faustus of Riez, the mid-sixth-century Britons Gildas and Vinniau, the late-sixth-century Irishmen Saint Columba of Iona and Mo-Sinu maccu Min and Saint Columban of Bangor, and a host of seventh-century Cambro-Latin, Hiberno-Latin, and Anglo-Latin authors, as from the epigraphic tradition illustrated by scores of inscribed stones from the fifth, sixth, and seventh centuries, that after withdrawal of Roman military and civilian administrators in A.D. 410 the Church maintained in these islands schools that produced writers capable of thinking and writing in literary Latin of a high register. By the seventh century the library of Insular Latin included works on grammar, prosody, computus, exegesis, hagiography in prose and verse, historical and topographical and devotional and cosmological poetry, canon law, and considerations of the physical nature of the universe, compositions serious and parodic, that in variety and volume and brilliance had no equals in any other part of Latin Europe. That is the milieu from which these charters emerged. These charters may help us to understand more clearly the character and behaviour of particular men as well as the course of Insular intellectual history.

Bede's account of the conversion of the English suggests that Augustine and the other missionaries sent by Pope Gregory the Great were not imaginative men of independent minds.[2] They tried to abandon their mission to the English even before they arrived in Lérins. Once in Britain they did not behave sensitively with British bishops.[3] The Latinity of a letter written by the Canterbury missionaries to Irish bishops, like that of a letter from the papal curia to Irish bishops, compares unfavourably with the Latinity of Insular scholars of

1 R.S.O. Tomlin, 'A Five-Acre Wood in Roman Kent' in *Interpreting Roman London, Papers in Memory of Hugh Chapman*, ed. Joanna Bird, Mark Hassall, and Harvey Sheldon, Oxbow Monograph LVIII (1996), pp. 209–15.

2 See Bede, *Historia Ecclesiastica* I XXIII–II XX.

3 *Ibid.* II II.

the same period.[4] The very nature of the questions posed to Gregory in the *Libellus Responsionum*[5] suggests that the missionaries wrote not from the barbarian Ruritania they may have supposed they were sent to, but from a culture in which polished Latinity and practised Christianity were not unknown. The questions imply the existence of deeply ascetic, Levitically oriented Christians, whose interests are not unlike those implied by canons in the penitentials of Insular Celtic churches of the fifth, sixth, and seventh centuries.[6] That every English kingdom converted by these missionaries lapsed, while those converted by Insular Christians remained faithful, occasions little surprise.

When Theodore of Tarsus, sent by Pope Vitalian as Bishop of Canterbury, arrived in 669, he repeated none of Augustine's mistakes. Armed with metropolitan archiepiscopal authority, perhaps by Pope Agatho as late as 678, he divided huge English dioceses into smaller units, to make them more like small Mediterranean dioceses centred upon cities, more like small Irish dioceses centred upon the *tuath*. Theodore included Irish pupils in his school at Canterbury.[7] Three separate attempts recorded in the *Leiden Glossary* to explain words from Gildas *De Excidio Britanniae* suggest that the syllabus of the school at Canterbury included Insular Latin texts, as do quotations from both Gildas and Hiberno-Latin poets in the works of Theodore's most illustrious pupil Aldhelm.[8] Employment of Old English words in the Biblical commentaries from the school at Canterbury,[9] and of scripts already used in these islands, notably uncial, half-uncial, and minuscule,[10] and of the Insular convention of separating words by space in manuscripts,[11] and of the Insular style of illumination in books produced in the school at Canterbury,[12] all suggest sensitivity to established Insular customs.

4 For texts of the letters see *ibid.*, II IV and XIX, and 'Insular Latin Writers' Rhythms', pp. 67–9.
5 Bede, *Historia Ecclesiastica* I XXVII.
6 *The Irish Penitentials*, ed. and transl. Ludwig Bieler, *Scriptores Latini Hiberniae* V (Dublin Institute for Advanced Studies, 1963).
7 'Insular Latin Writers' Rhythms', pp. 93–8.
8 See Howlett, 'Aldhelm and Irish Learning', pp. 38, 55, 'Seven Studies', pp. 54–7, *British Books in Biblical Style*, pp. 106, 122, *Cambro-Latin Compositions*, pp. 49–52, and 'Insular Acrostics, Celtic Latin Colophons', *Cambrian Medieval Celtic Studies* XXXV (1998), pp. 27–44.
9 For an index of these words see Bischoff and Lapidge, *Biblical Commentaries*, p. 588.
10 See above, pp. 13, 39, 42–3, 56; Webster and Backhouse, *The Making of England*, nos 64a–b, 79; *Cambro-Latin Compositions*, p. 161 and n. 14.
11 See the facsimiles of Durham, Cathedral Library, MS A.II.10, written about 650, and Hlothhere's charter of 679, above pp. 13–14 and n. 1, and E.A. Lowe, *Codices Latini Antiquiores*, vol. II ed. 2 (Oxford: Clarendon Press, 1972), no.*147 p. 9, Carl Nordenfalk, *Celtic and Anglo-Saxon Painting, Book Illumination in the British Isles 600–800* (London: Chatto and Windus, 1977), p. 32 and pl. 1, J.J.G. Alexander, *Insular Manuscripts, Sixth to Ninth Century*, A Survey of Manuscripts Illuminated in the British Isles I (London: Harvey Miller, 1978), pl. 10, Webster and Backhouse, *The Making of England*, no. 79.
12 The Insular style of illumination appears already developed in the Latin Gospels in Durham MS A.II.10, written about 650. Elements of this style feature in the oldest

This may help to explain why the seventh-century English charters are so unlike charters from the Continent. Theodore may have incorporated into English diplomatic practice some conventions shared earlier among the Welsh and the Cornish and the Irish, but illustrated only in documents extant from periods later than the earliest English charters.

Though all the texts considered in this book issued from the same tradition of thought and composition, the same matrix of Biblical style, the English, Welsh, Cornish, Irish, Scottish, and Hebridean charters are all distinct, and even within the local traditions the compositions are utterly idiosyncratic, no two being identical. The craftsmanship, one might fairly claim the art, of the documents suggests a higher level of education in these islands, and habits of intellectual abstraction both more intense and more generally diffused among a class of literate men larger than many have yet imagined.

None of the early documents considered here refers to a seal, nor does any of them bear traces of a seal nor autograph signatures nor autograph signs manual. From the period after the Norman conquest, when both seals and autograph signs manual became common,[13] in the charter of Duncan II of 1094, the charter of David I of 1124, the charter of Diarmait mac Murchada of 1162 x 1165, and the charter of Reginald that survives in a notarial instrument of 1426, seals guaranteed the authenticity and integrity of the documents to which they were attached, first supplementing and then replacing the structural devices embedded in the documents by composers and perceived by readers in acts of intellectual abstraction. With a dramatic increase in numbers of diplomatic documents during the twelfth and thirteenth centuries came greater reliance upon established formularies, a mass production different from the uniqueness of each document analysed in this book.[14] Yet even the last document considered here reveals a fifteenth-century Glaswegian notary as having understood completely the principles that informed the twelfth-century charter he examined and reproduced. In the apparent, as distinct from actual, symmetries with which his notarial paragraphs surround the reproduced original he shows that he also understood completely the injunctions of the *Rhetorica ad Herennium* from the very beginnings of the history of Western rhetoric.

extant historiated initials in *The Vespasian Psalter*, ed. David H. Wright, Early English Manuscripts in Facsimile XIV (Copenhagen: Rosenkilde and Bagger, 1967); Webster and Backhouse, *The Making of England*, no. 153.

13 For autograph crosses of William I and Mathilda see the charter of Waleran son of Ranulf in V.H. Galbraith, 'The Literacy of Medieval English Kings', The Raleigh Lecture on History, *Proceedings of the British Academy* XXI (1935), pp. 201–38, facsimile between pp. 200–1.

14 For facsimiles see T.A.M. Bishop, *Scriptores Regis* (Oxford: Clarendon Press, 1960); L.C. Hector, *The Handwriting of English Documents*, ed. 2 (London: Edward Arnold, 1966); Pierre Chaplais, *English Royal Documents, King John — Henry VI, 1199–1461* (Oxford: Clarendon Press, 1971); *Idem, English Medieval Diplomatic Practice, Part II Plates* (London: HMSO, 1975).

It would be idle to suppose that the documents we have considered here illustrate the only tradition of diplomatic composition practised in these islands from the seventh century to the fifteenth, idle to suppose that even within this one tradition we have done more than scratch the surface. This book is offered as an introduction, a challenge to abler linguists and better diplomatists, an invitation to those of sharper sight and keener hearing, a plea to those of deeper insight, to recover more of an intellectual inheritance that is already rich, but less precious than it was once and might be again.

in festo Sancti Dionysii
Anno Domini MCMXCVIII
Oxoniae

INDICES

I. INDEX OF MANUSCRIPTS

II. INDEX OF FACSIMILES

1867	Cosmo Innes and Sir Henry James, *Facsimiles of the National Manuscripts of Scotland* (Southampton: Ordnance Survey)	
	vol. I pl. II	89–90
1873	*Facsimiles of Ancient Charters in the British Museum* (London: British Museum)	
	pl. 1	13–14
	pl. 2	43–4
	pl. 3	47–9
	pl. 4	42
1878	John T. Gilbert, *Facsimiles of National Manuscripts of Ireland* (London: HMSO)	
	part II pl. LXII	81–3
1884	W. Basevi Sanders, *Facsimiles of Anglo-Saxon Manuscripts* (Southampton: Ordnance Survey)	
	vol. III pl. 1	39–40
1893	*The Text of the Book of Llan Dâv Reproduced from the Gwysaney Manuscript*, ed. J. Gwenogvryn Evans and John Rhys (Oxford, rept National Library of Wales, 1979)	
	pl. opp. p. xliii	61–2
	pl. opp. p. xlv	64
	pl. opp. p. xlvi	66–8
1911	P. Hume Brown, *History of Scotland to the Present Time* (Cambridge University Press)	
	vol. I pl. XIV	89–90
1913	*Liber Ardmachanus: The Book of Armagh*, ed. John Gwynn (Dublin: Royal Irish Academy)	
	frontispiece	79
1923	*Liber Vitae Ecclesiae Dunelmensis: A Collotype Facsimile of the Original Manuscript*, ed. A. Hamilton Thompson, Surtees Society CXXXVI	
	vol. I f. 48v.	87
1935	V.H. Galbraith, 'The Literacy of Medieval English Kings', The Raleigh Lecture on History, *Proceedings of the British Academy* XXI, pp. 201–38	
	facsimile between pp. 200–1	103 and n. 13
1937	*Book of Armagh, The Patrician Documents*, ed. Edward Gwynn, Facsimiles in Collotype of Irish Manuscripts III (Dublin: Irish Manuscripts Commission)	
	fol. 16v	79
1957	*Textus Roffensis*, ed. P. Sawyer, Early English Manuscripts in Facsimile VII (Copenhagen: Rosenkilde and Bagger)	
	vol. I fols 1–3v	55 and n. 43

III. INDEX OF ENGLISH AND CORNISH CHARTERS

P.H. Sawyer, *Anglo-Saxon Charters, An Annotated List and Bibliography* (London, 1968)
W. de Gray Birch, *Cartularium Saxonicum*, 3 vols (London, 1885–99).

IIII. INDEX OF 'A BIBLIOGRAPHY OF CELTIC-LATIN LITERATURE 400–1200'

V. INDEX OF DATES